THE SONG OF THE SERVANT

★

Bernard Häring, CSsR

The
SONG
of the
SERVANT

Biblical meditations on Mary,
the Mother and Model
of the Church

 St Paul Publications

ST PAUL PUBLICATIONS
SLOUGH   SL3 6BT   ENGLAND

Copyright © Bernard Häring 1977
Nihil obstat: D.A. Valente ssp
Imprimatur: F. Diamond vg, Northampton
First published November 1977
Printed in Great Britain by the Society of St Paul, Slough
ISBN 0 85439 143 6

CONTENTS

ACKNOWLEDGEMENT

I should like the reader to know my gratitude to Sr Joyce Gadoua and Miss Phyllis LaVoie, not only for typing and re-typing, but also for their competent help in caring for correct English.

B. H.

INTRODUCTION

The Second Vatican Council has crowned the Dogmatic Constitution on the Church with a beautiful chapter on Mary, the prototype and model of the Church. The Church cannot come to a full understanding of her union with Christ and her service to his gospel without a profound love and knowledge of Mary, the mother of our Lord and ourselves. Unfortunately, after the Council, many people in the Church did not give proper attention to this chapter.

Our veneration and love of Mary must not be minimized or de-emphasized, but, rather, renewed and deepened. Too much attention to private revelations and doubtful apparitions of the Blessed Virgin helps neither the cause of Christian unity nor our own love of Jesus. In these meditations, therefore, we shall turn our attention primarily to holy scripture and to the liturgy.

We venerate in Mary, the Queen of the prophets and apostles, the courageous woman, the humble handmaid of God and men, the one who lives fully the new law of the beatitudes. Through all that she is and tells us, she leads us to Christ.

If our veneration of Mary is authentic, then we can hope for a new springtime of evangelization, and progress in the cause of Christian unity.

I

MARY, A SIGN OF HOPE

In the midst of a male-centred culture that looked down upon women, the first pages of holy scripture underline the equal dignity of man and woman. 'Then God said, "Let us make the human person in our image, after our likeness" . . . so God created the human person in his image, in the image of God. Male and female he created them' (Gen 1:26-27). Woman and man together have this great mission to be for each other, an image of God: of his fidelity, his goodness, his tender love. We can only cry out in pain seeing that both betrayed their dignity instead of receiving each other as a gift of God and praising him together. They become self-centred and conceal God more than they reveal him. Yet, God's promise is with them from the beginning. There will come a new Adam and a new Eve. The woman is a sign of hope: 'The Lord said to the serpent: "I will put enmity between you and the woman, between your seed and her seed: he shall bruise your head, and you shall bruise his heel" ' (Gen 3:14-15).

The victor over arrogant and evil spirits will be Jesus Christ, the new Adam, but the promise of the Saviour is introduced by the image of the humble and courageous woman who is set as a sign against the evil one, against all those who in their arrogance and pride refuse to adore God and are unable to love their fellowmen. God promises the woman who will be a true image of God that her offspring will manifest all the goodness and faithfulness of God. He will be the visible image of the invisible God, and the new Eve will be his companion in her humility and purity.

In a time of great distress, the prophet Isaiah, inspired by the Spirit of God, invites the King of Judah to ask for a sign that God will set his people free. However, the king refuses to believe and to pray for a sign. And yet God promises through his prophet: 'The Lord God himself will give you a sign. Behold, a virgin shall conceive and bear a son and she shall call his name Emmanuel' (Is 7:14). In Israel, it was the right of the father to give a name to the son. It is an astounding privilege that a woman will give to the promised Saviour the name Emmanuel, that is, God with us. God will be with her — 'The Lord is with you'. She will experience, in a unique way, the nearness of the Lord. All her being spells out for us: 'The Lord is near'.

Still referring to the great prophecy that perceives a virgin who will give birth to the One whom she will call Emmanuel, Isaiah offers the glorious vision of the future Redeemer: 'To us a child is born, to us a Son is given; and the government will be upon his shoulder, and his name will be called Wonderful Counsellor, Mighty God, Everlasting Father, Prince of Peace, and of his reign and of his peace there will be no end' (Is 9:5-7).

We can hardly doubt that in the family of Mary these promises were frequently meditated upon and that, together, they sang the great songs of second Isaiah on the servant of Yahweh theme. As the virgin was for centuries a sign of God's promise to his people, so Mary, under the guidance of the Holy Spirit, lived the hope and expectation of Israel. Her whole life becomes the fervent prayer of the long advent: 'Shower, O heavens, from above and let the skies rain down righteousness; let the earth open that salvation may sprout forth, and let it cause righteousness to spring up also; I, the Lord, have created it' (Is 45:8). Before Mary received the message of the angel that she was the chosen one, she, the fairest daughter of Sion, must have prayed daily that the womb of the promised woman might open and salvation might spring forth. The Lord's promise and blessing was with her before she could know that she was the one chosen to give the wonderful name to the Messiah, 'Emmanuel', 'God with us'.

Mary surely lived most intensely the charism of the virgin who lives fully in vigilant waiting for the coming of the Lord. St John, who was entrusted by Jesus to Mary, and to whom Mary was entrusted, is the embodiment of the special charism of the virgin. He is 'the man waiting for the coming of the Lord' (cf. Jn 21:20-23). This charism is given in the highest way to Mary. The oil in her lamp is burning; all her being longs for the Lord, in readiness to greet him when he comes.

If we want truly to venerate Mary, the great sign of the promise, the new Eve, then we should above all appreciate the charism of vigilance and readiness. Man and woman in their complementarity should follow the new Adam and Eve, trying to become more and more fully an image and likeness of God, making visible for each other the presence of God: 'God with us'.

The Lord comes day by day through so many gifts and in the needs of our fellowmen. He calls us and urges us to be with him and to honour his coming. Blessed are we if we follow Mary in her vigilance and readiness.

We praise you, God, Almighty Father,
for having given in the Virgin
to your people and to all humankind
the great sign of hope for the coming
of the One who will make you fully visible to us,
    the Emmanuel.
We pray that daily we may live with Mary,
hope in gratitude,
and ever be vigilant in the readiness to respond
with all our being
to your calling and your gracious coming.

O Mary, whenever I remember you and call upon your
    name,

I feel hope in me and long to know with you the
Emmanuel,
the experience of God's nearness.
I thank you for your fervent prayer, for your longing
that was fulfilled in the coming of the Saviour.
Pray for us,
that our lives may be a constant thanksgiving for his
coming,
and become for many
a sign of hope, of trust, and an invitation to seek the
Lord. Amen.

II

FULL OF GRACE

'The angel Gabriel was sent from God to a town in Galilee called Nazareth, with a message for a virgin betrothed to a man named Joseph, a descendant of David. The girl's name was Mary. The angel went in and said to her: "Greetings, most favoured one; the Lord is with you". But she was deeply troubled by what he said and wondered what this greeting might mean. Then the angel said to her: "Do not be afraid, Mary, for God has been gracious to you; you shall conceive and bear a son and you shall give him the name, Jesus"' (Lk 1:26-31).

The fullness of time has come. The sign of the promise, the virgin, is now manifest to us; we know her name: Mary — the privileged name of God's design, a name that fills our heart with trust and joy.

With God's angel we say, 'Greetings to you'; this is the same as our 'Hail Mary' which we might also translate 'Rejoice'. God himself invites Mary to rejoice in the coming of the messianic era. How could she not rejoice knowing that she is the promised sign that announces the coming of the Prince of Peace. Whenever we greet her with the *Hail Mary*, we are joining her in her joy and gratitude.

'Full of Grace', God has graced her. She belongs totally to the Servant of Yahweh of whom the Lord spoke by the prophet: 'Behold my servant, whom I uphold, my chosen one on whom my favour rests' (Is 42:1). She has found favour before the Lord in view of him who is the beloved Son. The words that come from God in greeting are mighty; we may say they are an effective sacramental sign. God pours out into the heart of Mary the messianic joy; she

13

is the first to have a foretaste of the coming of the messianic age. Through a special revelation, Mary comes to know that she is a sign of hope, a sign that God fulfils his promises to Israel. Her whole life sings of God's faithfulness: 'Firm in his promise to our forefathers, he has not forgotten to show mercy to Abraham and his children's children forever' (Lk 1:55). From beginning to end, the life of Mary is graced; for she renders thanks always and everywhere, and thus she is open to experience the Lord's graciousness and to respond with generosity and ever greater gratitude.

Grace (*charis*) is not a thing; it is God's attractive love: God himself, turning his countenance to us, manifesting his love to us, in order to draw us to his heart. And no other person who lived prior to Mary has ever been so closely drawn to the heart of God as she. From her earliest youth, as she meditated upon the great messianic prophecies and all the events of the history of salvation, each word must have spoken to her of the attractive love of the Lord.

'The Lord is with you'. Now the great moment of history has come when the virgin will learn and understand in a unique way the name 'Emmanuel', 'God with us'. The Lord is with her, and she who is the daughter of Israel, the promised of all nations, does not think only about herself. Rejoicing in the presence of the Saviour, she calls him God with *us*, in view of *all* of us. Her joy in the presence of the Saviour is our joy, and we join her in her praise and thanksgiving.

'Do not be afraid, Mary'. The experience of God's presence and the revelation that the moment of fulfilment of the ancient promises had come must have shaken Mary's whole being. In her humility, she would not have allowed herself to think herself to be the promised virgin. Now God reveals himself and his designs to Mary. Her heart overflows with joy, and yet, she is shaken by her holy fear of God. This is the decisive moment in which Mary finds, on an even deeper level, the already existing synthesis of joy and awe, of rejoicing in the Lord's nearness and of praising his holy name.

Our own spiritual life cannot be healthy without the contrast and harmony of these two poles of joy and holy fear. In Mary, the fear of God cannot be that of an unwilling slave, but the fear of the daughter of God. And yet, surprised by the newness of the revelation, she needed a special help from God to overcome all fear and entrust herself totally to him, so that she could really touch the grace she had found before him. From beginning to end, she remains in the Lord's grace, for she is forever humble, grateful and faithful.

We praise you, Father, Lord of heaven and earth;
for what remains hidden from the wise and arrogant
you have revealed to the humble handmaid, Mary,
        the daughter of Sion.
You have chosen her to be the queen of the prophets,
and all this you have done for us.
Grant that we may always praise your name
by the veneration of the one you have chosen
to be the mother of your only begotten Son made man.
By the intercession of Mary,
and in the name of Jesus, the Emmanuel, we pray
that we too may experience his presence and come to
        know his name, 'God-with-us',
and rejoice in him who is the great sacrament of your
        nearness to us.

O Mary, what a joy it is that we can greet you
with the words 'full of grace'.
The favour you have found is for all of us;
the Lord, who is with you, comes to be with all of us.
We shall experience it if, like you, we are grateful
        and faithful.
Pray for us
that we may always be able to rejoice in the Lord's
        presence. Amen.

III

'YOU SHALL CONCEIVE AND BEAR A SON, AND YOU SHALL GIVE HIM THE NAME, JESUS'

The revelation is clear. Mary cannot doubt that she is the sign that is promised, the virgin who calls her Son, 'Emmanuel', 'God-with-us'.

Mary, the most humble among the humble, the holiest among all the saints, believes with the humble ones of the countryside that the promised Messiah will be the 'Servant of God'; and through special revelation and grace, she comes to know the great mystery: the One whom she will call Jesus ('God our Saviour') is the Son of the Most High and his reign will have no end.

She is the mother privileged to give him the name, a name which she experiences within her being. As mother, she will sing the praise of the Servant of God. As mother, she will give him loving care, and as believer, she will adore him.

Mary, the new Eve, the daughter of Sion, shares with her people the grateful memory of all the wonderful things God has done for Abraham, Isaac, Jacob, David and all his descendants. The memory now becomes a total celebration of gratitude for all that the Lord has already done and promised and now brought to fulfilment in her Son, who will reign in the house of Jacob and become the Saviour and Lord of all the world. Each word of the angel is inspired by the messianic prophecies of the Old Testament, and the memory and heart of Mary were filled by these prophecies which she must have meditated upon so

16

frequently with her family and friends, and in solitude. The promises would resound in her heart all the time.

Now, through the special grace of the Holy Spirit, all that has happened reaches its summit. It becomes for her, and through her, God's self-bestowal on humanity. She gives herself totally to him who is so gracious.

Mary is immaculate. She has not, like us, the need of ongoing purification. Her life, marked by the law of growth, is more so than that of others. Her faith becomes a more and more glorious light. In her openness to the divine message and the gift of herself, she becomes more and more intensely grateful and full of joy. The Lord God has guided her, step by step, to the moment in which she conceives the Son of the Most High. His grace has prepared her heart, soul, body, will and emotions. So prepared is her faith that her response and gift of self are the fullness of joy.

Unlike Zechariah, Mary has no doubts that the revelation will be fulfilled. Yet she has humbly to pray and to ask God in order to know what her co-operation in this wonderful event will be: 'How will this happen? I am still a virgin' (Lk 1:34). It is the prayer of the one who, like all of us, lives in faith, but with a fullness and sincerity that makes her the model of the Church. She teaches us how to search for nothing other than to know and to do the will of God.

Mary, although betrothed to Joseph, knew deep in her heart that she was not destined for a conjugal love in the common sense. This is, at least, suggested by the sacred text. We do not know whether she had made a vow of virginity, or simply received an intuition that virginity would be the road which, for her, would be the sign and promise. But one thing *is* clear: Mary is total openness to the will of God. She anticipates, in faith, the prayer of her Son: 'Thy will be done'. In that total gift of self it becomes clear to her, in mind and faith, that she is, in a total and permanent sense, the virgin who will call her Son, Jesus (God our Saviour), and Emmanuel (God with us).

17

We thank you, God our Father,
that through holy scripture and the faith of the Church
you have revealed to us that Jesus,
whom you have given to us as our Brother,
is the only One who has the birthright to call you
  Father,
having no Father on earth.
We praise your wonderful ways
by which you have guided Mary
and prepared her for faithful and grateful acceptance
  of your revelation
that she would be mother and virgin,
mother of your only-begotten Son.

O Mary, virgin and mother,
mother of the Son of God made man in you
and our mother also,
pray for us that like you
we may seek only one thing: the will of God;
that we may seek it with that humility and purity of
  heart
that distinguishes your faith. Amen.

IV

'BEHOLD, I AM THE SERVANT OF THE LORD'

The prophecies that are now to be fulfilled echo in the heart of Mary. 'Comfort my people, says our God. Speak tenderly to Jerusalem and cry to her that her time of slavery is ended. A voice cries: In the wilderness, prepare the way of the Lord, make straight in the desert a highway for our God. Every valley shall be lifted up, and every mountain and hill be made low; the uneven ground shall become level and the rough places, a plain. The glory of the Lord shall be revealed and all people shall see together, for the mouth of the Lord has spoken' (Is 40:1-5).

Now the hour has come, the hour to which the patriarchs and the prophets had looked. The fulfilment is greater than they could imagine. The angel says clearly how it will come about: 'The Holy Spirit will come upon you and the power of the Most High will overshadow you; and for that reason, the Holy Child to be born will be called 'Son of God' (Lk 1:35). This is the moment of a new creation by a wonderful intervention of the Holy Spirit. This is not the natural course of creation but a new manifestation of the power of the Most High, a manifestation greater than the creation of the universe from nothingness. This is the moment to which the earth can respond only with silence, adoration and everlasting thanksgiving.

To confirm the message for Mary, whose faith is already pure and strong, and to enhance our own faith the angel adds the message: 'Moreover, your kinswoman Elizabeth has herself conceived a son in her old age; and she who is reputed barren is now in her sixth month, for God's promises can never fail'. And yet the miraculous fecundity

19

of Elizabeth is only a small event in comparison to the unique newness which calls forth Mary's faithful and humble yes. 'Here I am', said Mary, 'I am the Lord's servant; as you have spoken, so be it'. It is clear to the faith of Mary, and to our own, that she is the companion of Christ, the Servant of God. As the new Eve, she gives her free and grateful assent. 'Here I am'. Thus, in Mary, the humble handmaid, comes to fulfilment the life and the prayer of all the prophets: 'Here I am, Lord; call me; here I am; send me'.

With that unreserved gift of herself, with that 'yes' of faith and fidelity, coincides the revelation of God's power. 'So the Word became flesh; he came to dwell among us, and we saw his glory, such glory as befits the Father's only Son, full of grace and truth' (Jn 1:14).

We adore you Almighty God and Father;
for in your great love you have wrought miracles
that no human mind ever
has thought possible or would have dared to hope.
Sending us your only-begotten Son you have given
        us everything
you could give us.
In him you reveal all your wisdom, your goodness,
        your gentleness and love.
We adore the One 'conceived by the power of the
        Holy Spirit'
and born of the Virgin,
as 'Light of Light, true God of true God'.
You have given him to us as our Redeemer,
as the Man for all men and as our Lord.
We give you thanks in the hope
that we shall be admitted to everlasting thanksgiving
in Jesus Christ, with Mary and all the saints.

O Mary, mother of our Lord Jesus Christ,
we thank you for your humble 'yes'.

You did not want to be anything other than a servant
of God,
following him who is the Servant of God and of all men.
We rejoice with you;
for the Most High has given you the honour and the joy
of being the mother of his Son since he has taken flesh
in you.
In our name, too, you have given the response of faith.
Pray that we too may respond
with all our heart, with all our being. Amen.

V

THE VISITATION

For Mary, to know that her kinswoman in her old age has conceived a son is a sufficient invitation to serve her. Mary's prayer, 'Behold the handmaid of the Lord', has, by necessity, a horizontal dimension. Simultaneously she is the servant of God and his gospel, and the servant of her neighbour. We find Mary not only in the house of Zechariah and Elizabeth in Ain Karen, but at Cana to help in the household and kitchen. How many times must she have felt an invitation by the Lord's grace to serve those needing her?

Mary meets Elizabeth and Zechariah as the servant of God. She comes to serve them but at the same time she comes to bring them the message of joy and peace. 'She went into Zechariah's house and greeted Elizabeth'. Her greeting is not only a courtesy, or a rejoicing in the meeting of old friends. She greets, as the daughter of Sion, with the age-old blessing and song of hope: *Shalom* — 'Peace'. It is a blessing, and in this moment the fulfilment of the hope of Israel. She bears in her womb the Prince of Peace, who has taken our human condition so that his joy and peace may shine in the hearts of all. He has come to establish a kingdom of peace and justice. Her coming and her greeting are signs of the coming and blessing of the Lord.

In our best tradition, the greeting among Christians was a praise of God and an exchange of blessing. Perhaps we can, ourselves, rediscover the meaning of the meeting of Christians in our own homes and among friends. How beautiful was the ancient greeting 'Praised be Jesus Christ', or, as it is heard in all of the areas in Italy where St Alphonsus worked: 'Praised be Jesus and Mary' — with the response — 'Praised forever'. Why have we lost this beautiful tradition? Perhaps it had become too formal, too routine. We need to learn anew how to praise God and bless each other in a more spontaneous way when we meet. Even a simple 'Good morning!' can be a prayer and a blessing.

The biblical text makes us consciously aware that Mary's greeting was a most powerful prayer and blessing. 'And when Elizabeth heard Mary's greeting, the baby stirred in her womb'. Through Mary, the one who is chosen to prepare the way of the Lord comes in contact with Jesus. His response is exultation, the sign of the peace and joy of the messianic age.

As John is stirred by joy, Elizabeth herself is truly blessed by the greeting of Mary. 'Then Elizabeth was filled with the Holy Spirit and cried aloud, "God's blessing is on you above all women and his blessing is on the fruit of your womb" '. In that favoured moment, Elizabeth received the Holy Spirit who inspired the prophets and made her discover the profound meaning of the visit of Mary. Her response is a blessing and a grateful affirmation of what God has done in Mary, who is that great woman in whom all generations will find the new Eve, who brings us the new Adam, Jesus Christ, the Saviour of all. Each time we say the *Hail Mary,* we join the angel and Elizabeth in praise for all that God has done in Mary.

'Who am I that the mother of my Lord should visit me?' John the Baptist humbly confesses that he is not good enough to unfasten the shoes of Jesus. With astonishment he will ask, 'Do you come to me? I need rather to be baptized by you' (Mt 8:14). With the same humility Elizabeth wonders how it can happen that the mother of her Lord comes to help her in her household. The coming of the servant of the Lord can be welcomed only with deep humility. The coming of Mary inspires veneration and awe: for blessed is he who comes in the name of the Lord.

In the house of the Visitation, we see a wonderful dialogue of faith, a shared prayer. There are five persons present: the eternal Word made man in the womb of the Virgin, his mother who brings the source of all blessing and peace, Elizabeth, filled with the Holy Spirit, the greatest among all the prophets who prepares the coming of Christ, John the Baptist and Zechariah, a man of deep silence but with opened eyes and heart. His silence is a true participation, listening and presence. The harvest will be his song: 'Praise to the God of Israel'.

Every Christian family and community is called to be a house of prayer and thus a source of joy for many. All of us will be helped to decipher the signs of the times and to discover the presence of the Lord when we gratefully share our faith and join in the praise of God.

Lord Jesus Christ, we thank you with Elizabeth, John
  and Zechariah
for your visit to their house;
and we thank you for all the times you have visited us
  in our lives
and in our families.
We thank you, Father Almighty,
for the coming of the greatest of all guests,
your only-begotten Son made Man for us.
He is your gift
but through your grace also a gift of Mary to us.
Grant to us that like Mary
we also may bring Jesus, his blessing and his peace,
to our friends,
to everyone we meet.

We thank you, Mary, with all the people
to whose houses you have brought the blessing and
  peace of Christ.
Bless us with your greeting, 'Shalom',
and pray for us that we may be attentive
to the many signs of the coming of Christ into our
  life. Amen.

VI

MARY, THE PROTOTYPE OF FAITH

'How happy is she who has had faith that the Lord's promise would be fulfilled'. We cannot offer any greater praise of Mary than that proclaimed by Elizabeth. Mary is the mother of the Church above all as the prototype of faith. Faith is the glad, grateful and humble acceptance of him who is the Way, the Truth and the Life.

Mary conceived in her womb the Incarnate Word of the Father when she received in her heart the good news of the coming of the Redeemer and the mission entrusted to her. Her response, 'Here I am, the Lord's servant', is faith filled with trust and hope. Her faith is total surrender and trust in God which engender an ongoing watchfulness for the signs of God's will, and bring forth love for the life of the world.

The faith of Mary is joy, but also a humble and eager searching for the will of God. In her faith, Mary can discern the signs of God's presence. She is a model for the Church in her synthesis of gratitude for God's undeserved gift and readiness to be of service to others. All the wonderful things of which the letter to the Hebrews speaks become an even greater song of joy when we think of the faith of Mary. 'Faith gives assurance to our hopes, and makes us certain of realities we do not see. It is for their faith that the people of old stand on record. By faith, we perceive that the universe was fashioned by the Word of God so that the visible came forth from the invisible' (Heb 11:1-3). In fullness of faith, Mary perceives the marvellous new creation that happens in the Incarnation of the eternal Word. It is the creation of the new earth and the new heaven, a creation more wonderful than that of the visible universe.

'Without faith, it is impossible to please God' (Heb 11: 6). Mary pleases God more than any other creature because she excels by her faith and trust in God.

'By faith, Noah, divinely warned about the unseen future, took good heed and built an ark to save his household. Through his faith, he put the whole world in the wrong and made good his own claim to the righteousness which come from faith' (Heb 11: 7). Through faith, Mary becomes for us the ark of salvation through which the Saviour of the world comes to us. She is the prototype of and the promise for the Church, who is the ark of salvation according to the measure of her faith.

'By faith, Abraham obeyed the call to go out to a land destined for himself and his heirs, to leave home without knowing where he was to go' (Heb 11: 8). In faith, Mary surpasses the faith of Abraham by far, and that of all the other patriarchs as well. She is ready to leave all of the usual patterns of life behind, setting out into a totally new and unknown land and accepting the mission to be mother and servant, the servant of the Saviour of the world. In faith-like obedience, she accepts the greatest exodus, that of Christ; the exodus beyond Egypt and the desert to that of the Cross.

'By faith, Abraham, when the test came, offered up Isaac: he had received the promises, and yet he was at the point of offering his only son' (Heb 11: 17). God did not want Abraham really to sacrifice his son. Through a deepened and more illumined faith, God freed Abraham and his offspring from the pattern of his former culture where so frequently the first born was sacrificed. God did not want the Jews and Pilate to kill his beloved Son, but he wanted Jesus, in whatever might happen, to make manifest his total readiness to give himself for the salvation of mankind. In his self-bestowal, he is totally followed by Mary, the servant of salvation. She joins, with a wounded but loving heart, the sacrifice of Christ on the Cross.

'And, what of ourselves? With all these witnesses to faith around us like a cloud, we must throw off every encumbrance, every sin to which we cling, and run with resolution the race for which we are entered, our eyes fixed on Jesus, on whom faith depends from start to finish' (Heb 12:1). Mary exceeds the faith of all other people because her total being turns to Jesus; she knows him as the Saviour of all and she gives herself totally to him who is the Servant.

It is in this way that Mary teaches us and all the Church. In all that she does and says, she reminds us there is no salvation in any other name save Jesus'.

We praise you, Father, source of all life and light,
for having sent us Jesus Christ, your Son,
Son of man, the son of Mary.
We thank you for having given Mary
a faith so pure, so strong, so full of joy,
that she became the most privileged messenger of
    salvation,
and the model of faith.
With Elizabeth and with the whole Church,
we praise the faith of Mary.
We praise you, the giver of all good gifts,
and the Holy Spirit who prompts the faith in our hearts.
We thank you for the new ark of salvation,
the Church that becomes visible in Mary, the prototype
    of faith
as the community of believers.
With the whole Church we look to her, the most pure
    Virgin,
who lives perfectly the integration of faith and life.
Trusting in her intercession we pray:
'Deepen our faith that each of us may be blessed because
    of our faith
and that we may always trust that your words will be
    fulfilled
in all who put their faith in you'.

27

O Mary, each time we pray, 'Blessed are you among women',
we praise you because of your faith.
Pray for us that our faith may always be strong and radiant,
filled with hope and readiness to become, with you,
a living gospel,
bringing the messianic peace to all people. Amen.

VII

THE SONG OF THE SERVANT OF GOD

'You, Israel, my Servant, Jacob, whom I have chosen, the offspring of Abraham, my friend; you whom I took from the ends of the earth, and called from its farthest corners, saying to you, "You are my servant, I have chosen you and not cast you off". I will help you, says the Lord; your Redeemer is the Holy One of Israel and you shall rejoice in the Lord; in the Holy One of Israel, you shall glory' (Is 41:8-16). This prophecy is fulfilled in Mary, the daughter of Sion, the crown of the history of Israel.

She is truly Israel, the servant, the humble handmaid who can sing the song of faith and joy, the song of the servant that will be fulfilled in Jesus, her son.

If we meditate on the songs of the servant in second Isaiah, and then upon the *Magnificat*, we see their spiritual unity. Thus, scripture tells us that Mary is the new Eve, Israel at its best, and she is truly on the side of the hoped for Messiah, the Servant of God.

Luke says with simplicity, 'And Mary said'. Surely Mary lived the song of the servant and shared it with Elizabeth and Zechariah. But, it is not merely a song in one great peak experience. These are words and prayer that are spelled out through the totality of her life, her thoughts, desires and actions. In the hours of joy and in the moments of suffering and even under the Cross, Mary's life will sing the song of the servant. Mary *is* the *Magnificat*. The apostolic community finds in this great song of praise the synthesis of the life and the role of Mary in the Church.

29

The *Magnificat* does not express only the personal faith of the Virgin and her most intimate union with God. It is the life-song of the one whom we rightly honour as the prototype and, as it were, the mother of the Church. Mary's life manifests what is meant to be the role of the Church throughout the history of salvation, enabling the Church to proclaim that God is on the side of the little ones. He it is who humbles the arrogant and exalts his Servant, Jesus Christ, and all those who follow him, after the example of Mary.

"Tell out, my life, the greatness of the Lord". Since the Greek text allows of two translations, it is equally acceptable to say, "Tell out, my soul, the greatness of the Lord". Surely it is the most intimate life in Mary that sings the song of the servant, but it is also her whole life. She is totally consecrated to the adoration and praise of God who manifests himself in the fullness of her life. Her being is thanksgiving. She is, with Jesus and because of Jesus, the perfect Eucharistic person. As adorer of the Father 'in spirit and truth', part of her thankful adoration is her sensitiveness to the needs of others and her desire to bring the good news of salvation to all people, thus honouring and praising God.

'Rejoice, rejoice, my spirit, in God my Saviour'. We could also translate: 'Rejoice, my spirit, in Jesus', for the name of Jesus, in Hebrew 'Joshua', means literally 'God my Saviour'. The spirit of Mary is touched and moved by the Holy Spirit. In her life is fulfilled the prophecy of Ezechiel: 'I will put my spirit in you' (Ez 37:14), and again 'and I will put my spirit within you and cause you to walk in my statutes and be careful to observe my law' (Ez 36:27).

Already the Fathers of the Church called Mary 'the bride of the Holy Spirit', for she is total docility and receives the gifts of the Holy Spirit with the most profound gratitude. She is the fullness of messianic joy and the most priviliged messenger of the glad news. Her faith is joy, and those who truly come in loving contact with Mary will experience the same joy of faith.

We praise you, Father Almighty,
for in Mary you have given us the new Eve, the strong
    Woman,
a sign of the new heaven and the new earth.
We praise you for having given Mary that fullness of
    faith's joy
from which flows the strength to serve you in all things.
We pray in the Name of Jesus your Servant,
followed by Mary, the humble handmaid:
'Let our whole life become an ongoing song of your
    greatness,
your holiness and mercy.
Grant to us a heart renewed;
cleanse us by the grace of the Holy Spirit
that we may always rejoice in you, Almighty Father,
and in Jesus Christ our Saviour'.

Thank you, O Mary,
thank you; for you have sung and lived the song of the
    servant,
the hymn of joy, in our name as well;
and you have prayed for us
that we may join you in the praise of God's greatness
and in the joy of being near to him.
And so we say 'thank you' together with all the saints
who in the new heaven and on the new earth
sing with you the praise of the Lord. Amen.

VIII

JESUS AND MARY: THE SERVANTS OF GOD

'Listen to me, o coastland, and hearken you people from afar. The Lord has called me from the womb of my mother; he called me by name and said to me, "You are my servant, Israel, in whom I will be glorified". And now the Lord who formed me from the womb calls me to be his servant, that I may bring Israel back to him, and that Israel might be gathered to him; for I am honoured in the eyes of the Lord, and my God has become my strength. He says, "It is too light a thing that you should be my servant to raise up the tribes of Jacob and to restore the remnant of Israel; I will make you a light to the nations, that my salvation may reach to the ends of the earth" ' (Is 49:1-6).

In the *Magnificat*, Mary shares her knowledge of the name of the Messiah, 'the Servant of God', with the Church, so that she, too, may come to know it more and more fully. She is worthy to sing the song of the Servant, for she herself is totally a servant of God and men. In her life's song, the Virgin proclaims the name of Jesus and makes him known as the light of the nations and the salvation of all the earth.

What remains hidden from the wise and arrogant, God has revealed to his humble servant Mary: the mystery of the kingdom that is proclaimed and brought into being by Jesus, the Servant. With great exultation, Jesus himself shares this truth with his disciples: 'At that favoured moment, Jesus exulted in the Holy Spirit and said, "I thank you, Father, Lord of heaven and earth; for what remains hidden from the wise and learned, you have revealed to the simple. Yes, Father, such was your choice". Then turning to his disciples, he said, "Everything is entrusted to me by my Father, and nobody knows who the Son is but the Father, and who the Father is but the Son and those to whom the Son may choose to reveal him" ' (Lk 10:22-23). I think we can rightly assume that in this great moment Jesus had in mind Mary, together with all who follow with her in the path of humility. Nobody comes closer to the mystery of the Servant than Mary; for she, the humble handmaid, knows that everything is a gift. 'So tenderly he has looked upon his servant, humble as she is. For from this day forth, all generations will count me blessed, so wonderfully has he dealt with me, the Lord, the mighty One'. She is blessed and worthy to be praised; for she is a servant, immaculate, totally free from the stain of arrogance, from all desire to put herself in the centre. Whoever turns truly to Mary and comes to know her, will, with her, turn totally to Christ, and will learn to know and to honour Jesus, the Servant, by the totality of his life.

Mary is the pure mirror, faithfully reflecting the grace of God. Therefore we praise the Lord over and over again in calling her blessed among women. However, our praise is truly adoration of God the Father, if the humility of Mary, who follows Christ the Servant, becomes the intention and purpose of our whole lives. When we truly come to know and to love Mary, we shall ask her to pray that the same gift of humility may be granted to us and received by us, so that the mystery of the kingdom of God can be revealed to us and through us.

We praise you, Father, Lord of heaven and earth,
for having revealed the name of Jesus, the name
    Emmanuel,
and his name, 'Israel the Servant',
to your humble handmaid, Mary,
from the time you called him in the womb of his mother.
We thank you, Holy Spirit, for having inspired
    the lifesong of Mary,

and for helping the infant Church to understand it;
for it is a light for our own life, a source of joy for all.
Come, Holy Spirit, and cleanse us from all arrogance
and pride.
Grant that we may not desire anything more
than to know the Father and the One he sent, Jesus Christ.
For that reason we also pray for the gift of humility;
help us that we may always be on the side of Jesus,
the Servant,
by being on the side of the downtrodden,
on the side of the humble,
to whom you reveal
the name of the Father and of his Son Jesus Christ.

We thank you, O Mary,
for the enchantment of your humility and joy.
Pray for us that we may be fully converted
to Jesus Christ, the Servant of God and men,
and thus be able to sing with you the song of joy
before Jesus, the Emmanuel. Amen.

IX

'WONDERFULLY HAS HE DEALT WITH ME, THE LORD, THE MIGHTY ONE'

'Sing for joy, O heavens, and exult O earth; break forth O mountains into singing; for the Lord has comforted his people and will have compassion on his afflicted. Can a woman forget her suckling child, that she should have no compassion on the son of her womb? Even these may forget, yet I will not forget you. Behold, I have graven you on the palms of my hands. Lift up your eyes round about and see; they all gather, they come to you. As I live, says the Lord, you shall put them all on as an ornament, you shall bind them on as a bride does' (Is 49:13-18).

In her boundless gratitude, Mary, whose whole life praises the greatness of God, is able to discover his wonderful works done in and for her, and for all of humanity. Only a lack of humility can make the human person unable to discover all the wonderful things God has done for him.

Mary has received the greatest sign of love and the greatest vocation that could ever be bestowed upon a mere creature. She is full of grace, strong in faith, and mother of the Lord, the new creation, the new Eve, and, through her, comes to us the new Adam, Jesus Christ. She is more than the first Eve, the mother of the living; God gathers his people around her to make them all one family in Jesus Christ.

Through a profound love of Mary, who herself sings of her joy and gratitude throughout her whole life, we learn to have a grateful memory and develop clearsightedness, so that we can see all the wonderful gifts God has bestowed upon us. We find our unique name with which

35

each of us is called by Almighty God. We come to a living faith in our vocation to holiness, a calling to the ministry of unity and peace. Whoever gratefully discovers all the gifts of God in himself will be equally able to discover the inner resources of others. We shall give credit and trust to our neighbour, and together we shall become more conscious that a divine artist, the Holy Spirit, is present in the midst of people for no lesser purpose than to make them a masterpiece of his love and wisdom. To refuse to see the good that God has so wonderfully done in us is a great sin against God, against oneself, and against one's fellowmen. From this blindness of ungrateful people comes, then, flight from responsibility and escape from reality by those who always live with 'if only'. Things are quite different when we learn to sing with Mary in joy and gratitude; in so doing, we also find courage and joy in responding to God's calling: 'Here I am Lord; call me; send me'.

The world around us as well as our own life becomes much more human and blessed as we learn to count the blessings of the Lord and share in the praises of his goodness. The consequence is that we discover thousands of wonderful things without wasting so much time with the chronicle of evil.

We praise you, Almighty Father,
for all the wonderful things you have done in Mary,
    your humble servant.
As her children, we praise you for making her the mother
    of the living,
perfectly configured to Christ your Son,
who has made himself freely the Servant of all people.
May we, with Mary, sing your wonderful deeds.
Develop in us a grateful memory for all that you have
    granted us.
Help us to discover the many signs
of the presence of your Spirit,
that we may more gratefully and generously co-operate
    with his grace

and become, more and more, an image of your goodness
and your compassionate love.

O Mary, we thank you for your life and your words
which teach us gratitude,
and teach us to discover all the wonderful things God
    has done for us
to the praise of his name,
making us ready to co-operate with his gracious calling.
    Amen.

'HIS NAME IS HOLY: HIS MERCY SURE
FROM GENERATION TO GENERATION
TOWARDS THOSE WHO FEAR HIM'

'And I will betroth you to me forever; I will betroth
you to me in righteousness and in justice, in steadfast love,
and in mercy. I will betroth you to me in faithfulness;
and you shall know the Lord' (Hos 2:19-20).

In Mary, the new Eve, God glorifies his name, that is,
his holiness and mercy. And Mary sums up all the songs of
Israel in the name of the new Israel, the universal people
of God chosen from all the nations; she sings the praise of
God who manifests his holiness by his mercy. She also
proclaims that God, because of his holiness, rejects the
arrogant, though his purpose is always to purify his people,
to show healing forgiveness and to make them holy. Mary
sees fulfilled the promise of the Lord: 'My heart recoils
within me, my compassion grows warm and tender. I will
not execute my fierce anger, I will not destroy Ephraim;
for I am God and not like a man, the holy one in your
midst, and I will not come to destroy' (Hos 11:8-9).

To Mary is given the sense of God in a striking way. In
the song of her life, there is a tension and harmony between
holy fear before all-holy God and trust in his compassionate
love. Mary, who is sanctified by the holy God from the
first moment of her life and who experiences God's sancti-
fying presence to the end, is herself a great sign of the
mercy of God, who, for the sake of Jesus, has protected her
from all contagion from the solidarity of sin. It is a sign
of spiritual health if both religious experiences, fear of

God and trust and joy in his mercy, are strong. Mary is the model of the Church, the model of all believers. The Church cannot be holy unless she constantly praises God's healing forgiveness and patience. Nor can she praise God's mercy towards her without showing compassion towards sinners, the poor and the outcasts. Where the Church follows Mary, her model, no one can be considered hopeless. The very fear of God's holy name prevents this kind of rigorism.

Those legalists who sacrifice the human person to the letter of the law, and who have no compassion on people, who, although showing good will, find themselves in irregular situations, do not know the holy name of God. The life and song of Mary are a commentary on the beatitude, 'Blessed are the merciful; mercy will be shown to them' (Mt 5:7). She is rightly praised as 'The mother of mercy'. She is the mother of One who is mercy incarnate.

We are justified and sanctified by God's undeserved justice, by his mercy. None can live in the new justice without the readiness to follow Christ in his generosity and compassion. Jesus, the reconciler, is honoured with Mary when healing forgiveness is shown towards our fellow-men; that is, when on all occasions people act as ambassadors of reconciliation and channels of peace. Thus united in the compassionate love of Christ, together, all can praise the holy name of God.

All-holy and all-merciful God,
grant that we may always honour your name in holy fear,
in trust and joy.
Let our whole life praise the mercy which you have
     shown to us,
and which you also wish to manifest to others
     through us.
Give us the courage to face our misery
in deep faith that your holy love can heal us.
Implant in us a grateful memory

39

that can never forget how often you have shown
    mercy to us,
and thus
enable us to be ready to forgive our brothers and sisters,
not only seven times, but seventy-seven times seven.
Make of us a living gospel of your holiness and mercy.

Thank you, O Mary, Mother of Perpetual Help.
Your immaculate holiness and your absolute humility
are the great challenge to us to turn away from all pride
and self-centredness,
and give the glory to God alone.
Thank you for comforting us by your song of God's
    mercy,
making us dare to go to the house of our Father and
    say 'Our Father'.
Pray for us that all our life may express childlike trust
in the merciful Father of all.
and that, at the same time, we may never forget that
    though he is near,
he is also distantly other from us;
that he is the holy One
and we, creatures and sinners, can come to him only
because he manifests his holiness through mercy. Amen.

XI

'THE ARROGANT OF HEART AND MIND HE HAS PUT TO ROUT'

'The deeds his own right arm has done disclose his might; the arrogant of heart and mind he has put to rout, he has brought down monarchs from their thrones, but the humble have been lifted high'. Here too, we see that Mary is inspired by the Old Testament's piety and profound vision of the history of salvation. 'To God, I commit my cause; who does great things and unsearchable, marvellous things without number; he sets on high those who are lowly, and those who mourn are lifted to safety. He frustrates the devices of the crafty, so that their hands achieve no success. He takes the wise in their own craftiness; and the schemes of the wily are brought to a quick end' (Job 5:8-13).

Our Lady of the *Magnificat* shows how false a privatized religion is. Mary is far from those who think only of personal salvation and spiritual comfort. Mary is the companion of the Redeemer of the world. She discovers the profound meaning of the history of salvation and especially the conflict between the Servant of God who honours the all-holy and all-merciful God, and the dragon, the arrogant spirit which manifests itself in overpowering people through misuse of authority and exploitation of the weak and the poor. As nobody else, Mary knows the conflict between two quite different messianic expectations in the people of Israel. The priestly caste and the mighty of the land expect a powerful Messiah, a national hero, who can submit all other nations to the power of the Jews. Even people of Nazareth and some of Mary's kindred along with those who begin to follow Christ as disciples are captives of these false expectations. On the contrary, Mary from the very beginning, sings with all her life, the true expectation: the Servant of God, the Messiah whom the Father sends will put the arrogant to rout; he opens the road of salvation to us by his humility emulated by Mary, the humble servant who is to stand under his Cross.

Each of us should examine his own life history in the light of the *Magnificat*, and especially in the light of this saving conflict in which Christ, the Servant, overcomes collective arrogance and pride. In this same perspective, the history of the Church should be studied. Visibly, she prospers and finds the assistance of God wherever she follows with Mary, the handmaid, Christ, the Servant. Through a spirit of humility and gentleness, the Church can draw to Christ the multitude of peoples. If with Mary and Joseph we sing the song of the Servant, we shall always better understand the profound meaning of the history of salvation. Before our eyes should always stand Jesus, who with Mary and Joseph and the *anawim*, lived his daily life in humility. It is the humble people who keep the world together; it is in them that Jesus continues to reveal himself.

When we listen to Mary's *Magnificat*, how different do we find her from the falsified pictures of inauthentic private revelations in which people believe that our Lady has revealed her manner of dress and made a criticism of the length of women's skirts! Mary is not a ritualist. She will never talk to people on meticulous questions, but she continues through the song of her life to speak to us on the great themes of salvation, on the humble exercise of authority, on concern for the common good, on justice and peace, and on respect for the weak and the oppressed.

We adore you, all-holy and almighty God,
for you have and will always put to rout the arrogant,
the oppressive and the unjust.
You will always be on the side of the oppressed,

the lowly and the outcast.
We praise you, for you have exalted your humble
    Servant, Jesus Christ;
you have given him a name above all names;
and you have exalted Mary, the humble handmaid,
to be the Queen of heaven.
You have made her a mighty prophet.

O Mary, how great are you, how glorious, how wonderful;
you have lived fully the mystery of salvation,
immaculately and uncontaminated by a lust for power.
Pray for us
that the Lord may keep us far from the temptation to
    arrogance,
vanity and exploitation of others. Amen.

'THE HUNGRY HE HAS SATISFIED
WITH GOOD THINGS'

'Arise up in splendour; for your light has come and the glory of the Lord has risen upon you. Nations shall come to your light and kings to the brightness of your rising. Lift up your eyes round about and see; they all gather together, they come to you. Your sons shall come from far and your daughters shall be carried in the arms. Then you shall see and be radiant, your heart shall thrill and rejoice. Your sun shall no more go down, nor your moon withdraw itself; for the Lord will be your everlasting light, and your days of mourning shall be ended. Your people shall all be righteous; the last one shall become the first, and the smallest one a great nation; I am the Lord; in its time I will hasten it' (Is 60: 1-21).

The *Magnificat* is a song of joy and gratitude for the fullness of God's graciousness and fidelity revealed in the messianic era. He responds to humankind's hunger and thirst for justice and salvation which his spirit has awakened. Those, however, who boast in their power and cling to their wealth cannot recognize the Servant of God, and consequently they go empty handed. Here again, the *Magnificat* comes close to the formulations of the beatitudes. 'Blessed are those who hunger and thirst for God's saving justice: they shall be satisfied' (Mt 5: 6). Mary is, with all her being, in the song of her life, the great teacher of the gratuity of salvation. Only those who honour God as God and render thanks for everything can receive his grace. With Mary, we profess our faith: 'we believe in the Holy Spirit, the giver of life'. God, in his superabundant freedom and love, wants to share with his created persons, his joy, goodness and wisdom. But God is holy. He cannot give himself to those who are arrogant in their making of God less than their primary purpose. Mary praises God with her whole life. Her spirit is filled with gratitude, and she is full of grace. In her humility and thankfulness, she is the prototype of the Church who, by her mission and through the power of the Holy Spirit, hungers and thirsts that God may be glorified by all men and that all may experience salvation. Mary, the queen of the prophets, warns us, however, against the terrible emptiness and frustration of those who are ungrateful. Where there is no gratitude, the gift is lost. The all-holy God cannot share himself with those who are unwilling to give him honour and to sing his praise with Mary. Thus Mary leads us again to a deep understanding of the first fundamental beatitude, that of the poor who stand before God fully recognizing that everything is his gift and therefore we are to rejoice, sharing the gifts of the one God and Father with each other. Before us stands Christ, who, infinitely rich, made himself poor, so that in him, we might be capable of sharing in the richness of God. And because he humbled himself in his great hunger and thirst to make us rich, the Father has glorified his name; he has given him the name above all other names.

We are called to nothing less than holiness. We are, through faith and baptism, a new creation. We can live united with Christ. But for all this, what is indispensable is the unceasing prayer through which the Holy Spirit awakens in us an ever-increasing desire for the fullness of holiness; a desire to live with Mary in the discipleship of Christ's humility and purity of heart according to that undeserved gift of justification which we have received from God.

We thank you, Almighty and all-merciful God, that for
  our salvation
you have sent your eternal Word

to become like us in all things but sin.
You so graciously turned your countenance
to those who have hungered and thirsted to honour you,
    to love you,
and to sing the praises of your Name.
We praise you for having revealed all your wisdom,
    might and glory
in your Servant, Jesus Christ,
and also for having manifested your graciousness in your
    humble handmaid, Mary.
We pray in his name, the name of him who is your
    Servant,
for the gift of humility and gratitude,
that we may open our hearts to your goodness
and to the wealth of your love.
Free us from our selfish selves, from the old man
    who is self-centred,
proud and totally void.
Purify us by the fire of your love
so that the sufferings and difficulties of our lives
may become for us a process of learning to hunger
    and thirst
only for your saving justice.

O Mary, full of grace,
in your heart, the hunger and thirst of Israel
and of all humanity
for salvation has come to fullness.
Therefore you are the blessed one who has experienced
    salvation.
Pray for us that in humility, gratitude and hunger
    and thirst
for God's saving justice,
we may prepare ourselves for the so-desired grace
    of a holy life. Amen.

XIII

GOD'S MERCY AND FIDELITY

'He has ranged himself at the side of Israel, his servant; firm in his promise to our forefathers, he has not forgotten to show mercy to Abraham and his children's children, forever'.

This again shows the rootedness of Mary's spirituality in the Old Testament. With great intensity, she lives the history of salvation. She surely had sung the great songs of the prophets long before she received the revelation that she was to be the virgin foretold by the prophets. 'In that day, this song will be sung in the land of Judah. We have a strong city; he sets up salvation as walls and bulwarks. Open the gates that the righteous nation which keeps faith may enter in. You keep in perfect peace those who have put their trust in you. Trust in the Lord forever; for the Lord is an everlasting rock. They shall live; their bodies shall rise. O dwellers in the dust, awake and sing for joy on that day: the pleasant vineyard, sing about it! I, the Lord, amidst your people, every moment, I water it' (Is 26:1-4, 19; 27:2-3).

It is Mary, the daughter of Sion, who sings of joy. The Word that has taken human nature in her is the great sign of God's faithfulness and mercy. But how could she not sing for joy and gratitude, since in her the great promises have been fulfilled? The One she bears as mother is the new Israel, the Servant, the Son of Man, the only begotten Son of God. From all corners of the earth, he will gather disciples who, with him and his mother Mary, can sing in gratitude the song of the new Israel. Those who, with Mary, follow the Servant of God and man,

47

will constantly experience God's mercy, his fidelity to his own name.

A key word of the Old Testament is 'covenant'. The *Magnificat* shows us that the spirituality of Mary is in accordance with covenant morality. She does not simply live as a private person. She lives before God in full union with those who expected the Messiah before her and with those who in generations to come will praise the Lord with her. She teaches us how to celebrate and to live the Eucharist. She possesses a grateful memory for all that God has done in the past, for the promises he has given since the time of Abraham. In Mary, the history of Israel comes to full life as she anticipates the life of the new Israel, the Church. In Abraham, God has blessed his offspring; blessed is Mary the woman promised at the beginning of the ages; for blessed is the fruit of her womb. Mary sings the song of Israel as the one who first experiences the fulfilment of the promises, and Mary, more than Abraham, becomes the model of faith for the new people of God.

After the *Magnificat,* we read the prosaic note, 'Mary stayed with her about three months and then returned home' (Lk 1:56). The evangelist wants to remind us that Mary, who so wonderfully sang the praise of God, representing the whole of history, is in the house of Elizabeth to serve in household and kitchen. She is, simultaneously, evangelist and handmaid. It is this humble girl to whom God has opened the horizons of the history of salvation.

Almighty and all-holy God, with Mary we praise your
    greatness,
for faithful to your own name as Father,
you have shown mercy to Israel and to all nations.
You have fulfilled your promises in love for Mary
through her Son, your Christ.
We pray for your people Israel
that they may be blessed and turn to Christ your Son.
Grant to us to whom you have given the new and
    everlasting covenant,

48

the grace to live in gratitude and fidelity,
praising your faithfulness.

O Mary, we thank you for the *Magnificat*,
for the song of your life
with which you have enchanted Elizabeth and
    Zechariah
and all who have met you.
We thank you, that in your life,
you have made visible the mercy and fidelity of God,
who has done such great things in you.
Pray for us that our gratitude may increase,
and that we may more and more appreciate the gifts
    of God,
so that our life, too, may become a song
praising God's mercy and fidelity. Amen.

XIV

MARY AND JOSEPH

'This is the story of the birth of the Messiah. Mary, his mother, was betrothed to Joseph; before their marriage she found that she was with child by the Holy Spirit. Being a man of principle, and at the same time wanting to save her from exposure, Joseph desired to have the marriage contract set aside quietly. He had resolved on this when an angel of the Lord appeared to him in a dream. "Joseph, Son of David", said the angel, "do not be afraid to take Mary home with you as your wife. It is by the Holy Spirit that she has conceived this child. She will bear a son, and you shall give him the name of Jesus (God is Saviour), for he will save his people from their sins". All this happened in order to fulfil what the Lord declared to the prophet: "the virgin will conceive and bear a son, and he shall be called Emmanuel", a name which means "God is with us". Rising from sleep Joseph did as the angel had directed him; he took Mary home to be his wife and she, without having intercourse with Joseph, gave birth to her son. And he named the child Jesus' (Mt 1:18-25).

It is easy to discover the intention of this passage from the gospel of Matthew. The main purpose is to affirm strongly the virgin birth. Christ is born of the Virgin Mary through the work of the Holy Spirit. He had only one Father, the Father in heaven. On the other hand, the gospel exalts the role of Joseph. Matthew traces his lineage back to Abraham, our father in faith; Joseph is presented as a man of unwavering faith and of great justice.

He was a 'just man'. To see that the virgin betrothed to him was pregnant must have caused him sleepless nights. And yet, he does not allow himself to utter suspicion or accusation. The decision he has worked out in his mind is not according to the written law or tradition but simply according to the law of love. On the basis of the legal dispositions, he would have had to hand a written declaration to the elders with the motives for his decision to repudiate Mary. This would have brought great pain to Mary. Feeling that he has no right to marry her, he finds a solution that would safeguard her reputation in a way that tradition could not. His anguish must have been as great as that of Abraham who thought he had to sacrifice his first born son, Isaac. Like Abraham, Joseph receives a revelation from the angel of God, a revelation that opens up totally new horizons.

He knows from the scriptures that the Virgin will give the name to her son, the name of Jesus. Now he is invited by God's angel to share in the privilege of the Virgin to experience the nearness of God in Jesus, the Saviour. He is given to Mary and Jesus as companion and support for the days of joy and for the crucial hours.

In him, the history of the patriarchs, which is a history of faith and exodus, is lived again. We might honour him, too, with the name patriarch; for in him who is just and strong in faith, the history of the patriarchs comes to its finest fulfilment. 'By faith, Abraham obeyed the call to go out to a new land destined for himself and his heirs, and left home without knowing where he was to go. By faith he settled as an alien in the land promised to him' (Hb 11:8-9). Joseph, too, accepts a mission that will lead him on to roads he does not yet know, but he will always travel on the way of faith, and for that he will receive abundant light, more abundant than Abraham's. At Mary's side, Joseph, considered by law as the father of Jesus, will play an active role in the history of salvation. In his humility and faith, he will know with Mary the name of Jesus, 'Emmanuel, God-with-us'. With Mary, he will sing

51

into the heart of Jesus the songs of the Servant, by word and deed.

Joseph will live without earthly security; arriving at Bethlehem, he will not find a home for Mary and for her son to be born; with Jesus and Mary, he will live, again, the history of Israel, a refugee people in Egypt. He will return to Nazareth putting his trust in God alone. From a total lack of earthly security will come to him the experience of God who is our rock. He teaches us how to live in faith and hope with Mary and Jesus.

The Church of today lives anew that stupendous exodus in the transition from one era to the next. Her people are losing many earthly securities while a number of human traditions are being shaken. In this situation, humankind can look to the Holy Family and learn that it is not for Christians to seek earthly securities but to find strength in faith. It is the purpose of the Church's life to manifest trust in the Lord, to live in his presence and know that God will abide in her. He alone is her stronghold and he will be with all who believe in him.

We praise you, holy God, for having brought to fulfilment
the history of the patriarchs in St Joseph,
whom you so graciously gave to Jesus and Mary
as companion and protector.
You blessed him with a strong faith and great trust
in you.
Through the intercession of Mary and Joseph,
we pray that you will always protect your Church
and bless her with the gifts of faith and trust.
Be with your Church, be with all of us,
that we may not lose heart in these testing times
of change,
indeed, of painful exodus.
May your Church live faithfully this period
in which the centres of influence are changing.

May she be a sign of fulfilment of the old promises,
for Africa, and Asia, indeed, for all cultures.

Mary and Joseph, we thank you
for having lived the moments of uncertainty and anguish
with purity of heart, with one desire:
to be faithful to the Lord.
The surprising and new ways of God made you seek
    new ways.
Though frustration was not spared you,
your faith was only strengthened.
Protect us by your intercession
that we may never forget the presence of our Lord
who is our joy and our strength. Amen.

XV

'SHE GAVE BIRTH TO A SON, HER FIRST-BORN'

'In those days, a decree was issued by the Emperor Augustus for a registration to be made throughout the Roman world. This was the first census of its kind; it took place when Quirinius was governor of Syria. For this purpose, everyone made his way to his own town, and so Joseph went up to Judea from the town of Nazareth in Galilee, to register at the City of David, called Bethlehem, because he was of the House of David by descent; and with him went Mary who was betrothed to him. She was expecting a child, and while they were there, the time came for her baby to be born, and she gave birth to a son, her first-born. She wrapped him in swaddling clothes, and laid him in a manger because there was no room for them in the house' (Lk 2: 1-7).

The great moment has come to which the whole world is looking. And at this hour, Mary and Joseph live the exodus, the pilgrimage of Abraham, Isaac, Jacob and the patriarch Joseph, of Moses and of the whole people with the greatest intensity. They anticipate the history of the pilgrim Church on earth.

In extreme poverty, but with faith and trust and a great love as their true riches, Mary and Joseph live this breathtaking moment of the history of salvation in a poor stall. The external circumstances should not distract from him who is everything in all things, who is the greatest gift of the Father to his creation. He is the child most wanted, most desired, most loved. And this child lying in a manger is the Prince of Peace, the King of kings.

This great moment reveals to us the true sense of poverty.

Mary and Joseph tell us one great truth: God alone suffices. What more could they desire than to know him whom God has called and whom they will call Jesus, Saviour, Emmanuel, God-with-us.

Jesus is called the first-born of Mary. This does not mean that she gave birth to other children. But it does include in its meaning that she who calls the only begotten Son of the Father made Man in her, her 'first-born', knows that in the new family Jesus will have many brothers and sisters. He is the first-born of all creation; in him, the eternal Word of the Father, are created all things, and all things were made in view of him who came into the world as the light and life of the world. He is the first-born; the only One who has the full birthright to call the eternal Almighty God, his Father. He is the only begotten Son and yet the first-born; for he wants to call us all to be his brothers and sisters and to join him in the cry of joy, 'Abba, Father'. It is in him that we can say, 'Our Father'. And it is also because of him that we have a right to call Mary, our mother.

O all-holy God, we kneel down and praise your wisdom.
We adore you in the first-born of Mary, in your
    only-begotten Son
in whom you have given us everything
and in whom you have entitled us to call you our Father.
We praise you, for you have manifested your fatherhood,
and the tenderness of your fatherly love,
by giving us Jesus as brother and Mary as our mother.
May all our life reflect your greatness,
and may our spirit rejoice in you and in the joy
    you gave us
in Jesus Christ.
Make us grateful.
May your Holy Spirit come upon us so that our whole
    lives
may become thanksgiving, wonder, adoration and praise
    of your name.

O Mary, how great must have been your joy in
   that moment.
Pangs of childbirth, the anguish of the exodus, the
   poverty of the stall
are only the background of your joy.
You have no other treasure but Jesus, your first-born;
and you have no other desire than to awaken trust in him
who is the Emmanuel, God-with-us, our salvation,
   our joy.
Pray for us
that we may obtain that poverty of spirit that allows
   us to find Jesus,
our only treasure,
our only love,
and to learn to love with him all for whom he came
   as Saviour.
Pray for us that we may put all our trust in him. Amen.

XVI

THE SHEPHERDS FINDING THE GOOD SHEPHERD

'Now in this same district, there were shepherds out
in the field, people keeping watch through the night over
their flock, when suddenly there stood before them an
angel of the Lord, and the splendour of the Lord shone
around them. They were terror-stricken, but the angel said,
"Do not be afraid; I have good news for you. There is great
joy coming to the whole people. Today in the City of
David a deliverer has been born to you—the Messiah,
the Lord. And this is your sign: you will find a baby lying
wrapped in his swaddling clothes, in a manger". All at
once, there was with the angel a great company of the
heavenly host, singing the praises of God: "Glory to God
in the highest, and on earth his peace to those on whom
his favour rests" '.

'After the angels had left them and gone into heaven
the shepherds said to one another: "Come, we must go
straight to Bethlehem and see this thing that has happened,
which the Lord has made known to us". So they went with
all speed and found their way to Mary and Joseph; and
the baby was lying in the manger. When they saw him,
they recounted what they had been told about this child;
and all who heard were astonished at what the shepherds
said. Mary treasured up all these things in her heart and
pondered over them. Meanwhile the shepherds returned
glorifying and praising God for what they had heard and
seen; it had all happened as they had been told'
(Lk 2: 8-20).

There is a profound meaning in the fact that God
revealed Jesus, the Son of Mary, first to the shepherds

through the song of the messianic peace. In this experience of Mary, there coincide two of the great messianic promises which she must have meditated upon throughout the years and which must have resounded equally in the heart of Joseph: that God himself would be the Good Shepherd, and that he would both be and bring us the fulness of peace. With the visit of the shepherds, who so fully joined her in the praise of the Lord and who became the first messengers of the coming of the Saviour, great prophecies would re-echo again in the heart of Mary and Joseph: 'Behold, the Lord God comes with might; with him is the rightful rule; behold, his reward is with him, and his recompense before him. He will feed his flock like a shepherd; he will gather the lambs in his arms; he will carry them in his bosom, and gently lead those that are with young' (Is 14:10-11).

'Thus, says the Lord, God: behold, I myself will search for my sheep, and will seek them out. As a shepherd seeks out his flock when some of his sheep have been scattered abroad, so will I seek out my sheep; and I will rescue them from all places where they have been scattered on a day of clouds and thick darkness. And I will bring them out from the peoples and gather them from the countries, and will bring them into their own land; and I will feed them on the mountains of Israel, by the fountains, and in all the inhabited places of the country. I, myself, will be the shepherd of my sheep, I will seek the lost and I will bring back the strayed, and I will bind up the crippled, and I will strengthen the weak, and the fat and the strong I will watch over; I will feed them in justice' (Ez 34:11-16).

Mary and Joseph have recognized in Jesus, God-with-us, the promised Good Shepherd who manifests to us the infinite love of God, our Father, who cares for his people. They rejoice in the simple shepherds who make Jesus known wherever they go. Mary and Joseph rejoice with the angels, for they know Jesus as the Prince of Peace.

More than anyone else, Mary knows that Jesus has not come to judge or to condemn but rather to seek the lost sheep and heal them. We need the mind of Mary and of the good shepherds in order to find Jesus, to rejoice with the angels, to sing his praise and proclaim his peace.

Mary treasures up in her heart the message brought by these good shepherds and the angels. And her meditation on Jesus the Prince of Peace, on Jesus the Good Shepherd, has surely a prayer for us, that is, that the Church may never be lacking 'good shepherds', shepherds shaped in the image of Christ, nor be without those who rejoice in the peace of Christ and share it with all people. When we celebrate these great events in the Eucharist, we need the grateful memory of Mary. We need to be thankful for the message which is brought to us so that we can be fully open to the grace and joy of the good news.

It is characteristic of St Luke, the great teacher of prayer, to terminate his account of every great event of the Nativity with a choral ending in praise of God. Everywhere the good shepherds proclaim the news of God and praise God. Mary's is the model of the song of praise; a genuine veneration of Mary will lead us to understand the Eucharist more fully. It will transform all our life into a *Magnificat*, a praise of God for the good shepherds.

We thank you, Almighty and all-holy God;
for in Jesus Christ, you have fulfilled your promises
that you yourself would be the Shepherd of your people.
Make us holy, make us one in your love that we may
better know Jesus,
the Good Shepherd,
and be always united with him.
Bless your Church, that she may always have good
shepherds
who know how to praise you and how to bring the
message of peace
to all people.
Create in us a great compassion for those lost,
that we may, like Mary and Joseph,

know you as the Good Shepherd
and may make you known to all people of good will.

O Mary, Mother of the Good Shepherd,
pray for us and pray for the shepherds of the Church,
that they may truly and fully know the name of Jesus,
the Good Shepherd,
so that their hearts,
filled with compassionate mercy for those who go astray,
may patiently seek them out and gently bring them
     home
into their Father's house.
Pray for us that gratitude may inspire all that we think,
desire, and do. Amen.

XVII

THE SIGN OF THE COVENANT

A great moment in the life of Mary is the event of Jesus' circumcision, a moment in which his name is solemnly proclaimed, Jesus—God our Saviour. It is the moment in which the covenant of God with Abraham and Moses is proclaimed in the one who is in himself 'the covenant of the people'.

'The Lord said to Abraham: "I am God Almighty. Walk before me and be blameless. And I will make my covenant between me and you and will multiply you exceedingly; and I will make nations of you, and kings shall come forth from you. And I will establish my covenant between me and you and your descendants after you throughout their generations for an everlasting covenant, to be God to you and to your descendants after you. And I will be their God. This is my covenant which you shall keep between me and you and your descendants after you: every male among you shall be circumcised, and it shall be a sign of the covenant between me and you. He that is eight days old among you shall be circumcised" ' (Gen 17:1-12).

For Mary and Joseph, the ritual of circumcision is a profound renewal of the commitment to the covenant and the law of the covenant, which is, above all, to love God with all our hearts, with all our souls and with all our energies, and to love our neighbour as ourselves. The ritual is a memorial event when the Israelites gratefully recall all that God has done in the past.

For Jesus, it is more than a remembrance of the past deeds of God. It is the fulfilment of the covenant God has promised to Abraham and his descendants; for with the coming of Jesus, begins the new covenant.

'I am the Lord, I have called you in righteousness, I have taken you by the hand and kept you; I have given you as a covenant to the people, a light to the nations' (Is 42:6). This is from the song of the Servant which must have been well known to Mary. Her spiritual life must have been thoroughly nourished by these songs. So she would know with heart and mind that one of the great names of Jesus is 'The Covenant of the people'. Jesus is the Man for all. He is incarnate solidarity, who thus establishes the law of saving solidarity for all. Mary knows in faith and absolute readiness that she is not meant to live solely for her own salvation; living with Jesus, who is the Covenant of the people, she is therefore thoroughly committed as the servant of salvation.

All of Jesus' life is a manifestation of the new covenant, but there are some solemn moments, one being the circumcision with the symbolic shedding of blood, the blood of the covenant. Another profound moment is the baptism of Jesus in the Jordan during a general baptism. In this way he manifests that he is ready to bear the burden of all, he who is the Covenant of mankind, the Light of all nations and the Servant of God. As he commits himself publicly, the Holy Spirit comes visibly upon him and the Father proclaims him as his beloved Son. All this is merely a liturgical preparation for the great moment when Jesus, already baptized with the Holy Spirit, receives the real baptism in his blood, which is and will always be the blood of the new and everlasting covenant.

We celebrate our baptism as sign of our insertion into the covenant. It becomes the full truth of our lives when we no longer live for ourselves but with Jesus who is the Covenant, and with Mary, the servant of the covenant, who help us to live for one another and bear the burdens of one another in saving solidarity. Each time we celebrate baptism, there is a spiritual presence of Mary who has lived, in a unique way, the transition from the Old to the New Testament. With Joseph, she is the qualified witness when Jesus received circumcision as a sign of continuity with the covenant God made with Abraham.

In baptism, solemnly, we receive the honour and the name of children of God. The name of Jesus was decided and even made known before he was conceived in the womb of his mother, but it is the privilege of Mary and Joseph to confirm and proclaim his name. This name *Jesus* is for us, always a prayer of praise and of petition: *God, our Saviour*. We put all our trust in him and thus praise his name and bless each other in the name of Jesus.

God of our fathers,
we praise you for the covenant
you made with humankind from the beginning,
for the covenant with Noah,
Abraham, Jacob, Moses and with all your people;
for these covenants are the promise
of the One who is the abiding Covenant, Jesus Christ,
your only begotten Son whom you have sent to be our
    brother,
bearing our burden
that we too may learn to bear the burdens of one
    another.
We thank you together with Mary
who has put all her trust in you
and who has, throughout all her life, honoured the
    name of Jesus.
We thank you for the sign of the new covenant,
the baptism that makes us sharers in the baptism
which Christ has received for us
in the Jordan and on the Cross.
During the baptism in the Jordan,
you manifested him as your beloved Son,
and at our baptism you assured us
that we can share in Christ's prayer
and can call you 'Abba', 'Father', 'Our Father'.
Let this prayer, each time we say it,

be our expression of fidelity to the covenant
and our gratitude for the blood of the new and everlasting covenant.

O Mary, how great must have been your joy
when, at the circumcision, you could proclaim the name
of Jesus,
whom you recognized as the Covenant of the people.
Pray for us that we may better understand
the meaning of the new and everlasting covenant,
and thus come to live fully, in fraternal love,
the birthright which baptism has given us. Amen.

XVIII

THE PRESENTATION IN THE TEMPLE

'Then after their purification had been completed in accordance with the law of Moses, they brought him up to Jerusalem to present him to the Lord (as prescribed in the law of the Lord: "every first-born male shall be deemed to belong to the Lord"), and also to make the offering as stated in the law: "a pair of turtle doves or two young pigeons" ' (Lk 2:22-24).

The presentation of Jesus in the temple was, like the circumcision, an act of obedience to the law of the old covenant, and thus at the same time, a prophetic gesture that announces the coming of the new covenant, that of the anointed one, Christ, the high priest and prophet.

God himself has, through Moses, explained the profound meaning of this act of presentation: 'The Lord said to Moses, "Consecrate to me, all the first-born. Whoever is the first to open the womb before the people of Israel is mine. And when the Lord brings you into the land of the Canaanites as he swore to you and your fathers, and shall give it to you, you shall set apart to the Lord all that first opens the womb. And when in time to come, your son asks you, "What does this mean?", you shall say to him, "By the strength of his hand the Lord brought us out of Egypt from the house of bondage" ' (Ex 13:1-14).

When Mary, in obedience to the law, fulfils this ritual, praising God for the liberation from the bondage of slavery, she knows that Jesus belongs to God the Father in a unique way. The ritual is only a manifestation of the deepest truth that Jesus, from the beginning, is totally consecrated to the kingdom of the Father and to the gospel. But it becomes gradually clear to Mary that the road which Jesus is to follow will demand from her detachment and great sacrifice. At the proper moment, she will humbly hide herself as John the Baptist will do, so that Jesus, in his uniqueness, may be manifested to all as the prophet, the priest, and the sacrifice.

The presentation of the first-born is an act of consecration. While Mary fulfils this act, presenting the one who is consecrated by the Holy Spirit, she consecrates herself as his companion and servant. She knows that the ritual sacrifice of a pair of turtle doves cannot be a substitute for the offering of herself. This is so especially in view of Christ who comes to offer himself.

At the baptism of Jesus in the Jordan, the dove becomes the symbol of consecration through the Holy Spirit. Mary, with the simplicity of a dove, is always faithful and docile to the promptings of the Holy Spirit, and thus fulfils her role in the work of redemption. Through the gifts of the Holy Spirit, she has, at every stage, an intuition of what the Lord asks of her, she who offered her first-born in the temple.

We thank you, Lord, God of history,
we thank you, that through Moses, your servant,
you have revealed to us the profound meaning of
        the presentation,
that came to its full truth in Jesus Christ,
the One who was expected by the prophets.
While Mary offered Jesus, she also presented herself,
with the one great desire to honour your name in
        all things.
Grant through her intercession
that when we offer Jesus in the Eucharistic sacrifice
we may also offer ourselves wholeheartedly to your
        service
with Jesus and Mary.

O Mary, present us with Jesus to the Father in heaven, pray for us that we may learn what a great joy it is to know that we belong to God as his property, consecrated to him together with your first-born, Jesus Christ. Amen.

XIX

QUEEN OF THE PROPHETS

'There was at that time in Jerusalem a man called Simeon. This man was upright and devout, one who watched and waited for the restoration of Israel and the Holy Spirit was upon him. It had been disclosed to him by the Holy Spirit that he would not see death until he had seen the Lord's Messiah. Guided by the Spirit, he came into the temple; and when the parents brought in the child Jesus to do for him what was customary under the law, he took him in his arms and praised God and said:

> "This day, master, thou givest thy servant his discharge in peace; now thy promise is fulfilled; for I have seen with my own eyes the deliverance that thou hast made ready in full view of all the nations: a light that will be a revelation to the pagans, and glory to thy people, Israel".

The child's father and mother were full of wonder at what was being said about him. Simeon blessed them and said to Mary his mother, "This child is destined to be a sign which men reject, and you too shall be pierced to the heart. Many in Israel will stand or fall because of him, and thus the secret thoughts of many will be laid bare".

'There was also a prophetess, Anna, the daughter of Phanuel, of the tribe of Asher. She was a very old woman who had lived seven years with her husband after she was first married, and then alone as a widow to the age of eighty-four. She never left the temple but worshipped day and night, fasting and praying; coming up at that moment, she returned thanks to God; and she talked about the child to all who were looking for the liberation of Jerusalem' (Lk 2:25-38).

The gospel of Luke presents Mary very clearly to us as the queen of the prophets. When she brings her greeting and blessing to the house of Zechariah, John, still in the womb, leaps for joy, and thus initiates his prophetic role of proclaiming the one who would baptize with the Holy Spirit. Elizabeth is filled with the Holy Spirit, and after a period of silence, Zechariah utters the great prophecy in a song similar to that of Mary.

Again, when Mary brings Jesus to present him in the temple, another astonishing encounter with the prophets happens. Around Jesus are four noble representatives of the *anawim*, the humble of the country. The outpouring of the Holy Spirit upon Elizabeth and Zechariah, on Simeon and Anna is a sign of the new messianic era. It becomes clear that God reveals himself to the humble and the simple. 'I praise you, Father, Lord of heaven and earth, for hiding these things from the learned and wise, and revealing them to the simple. Yes, Father, such was your choice' (Lk 10:21). Another word of Jesus finds fulfilment already: 'Happy the eyes that see what you are seeing. I tell you, many prophets and kings wished to see what you now see, yet never saw it; to hear what you hear, yet never heard it' (Lk 10:23-24).

Simeon and Anna are the privileged ones to whom God reveals the coming of the Messiah. Simeon and Anna are similar to Mary in the intensity with which they lived the expectation and hope of the coming Saviour. The encounter is an occasion for praising the Lord, and the revelation granted to this holy group becomes at once proclamation of the things to come. Simeon announces Jesus, not only as the liberator of Israel but also as the light of all nations, and Mary receives these prophetic voices of joy and praise and evangelization as the queen of the evangelists and apostles. She longs that everyone should know the Saviour.

Mary, too, receives a special prophecy, that of the sword

of suffering. She is the one who is to follow Christ wherever he goes, even to the abyss of suffering. Mary and Joseph as well as Simeon and Anna would have meditated on the fourth psalm of the Servant of Yahweh:

> 'He was despised and rejected by men, a man of sorrows and acquainted with grief. Surely he has borne our grief and carried our sorrows' (Is 53:3-4).

From now on, the participation of Mary in the mystery of salvation becomes clearer. More than the martyrs and the apostles, Mary shares in Christ's suffering. Because of her great love, she, in her immaculate heart, is to suffer more with Christ than anyone else. It is from Christ, however, that her share in the work of redemption has its great fruitfulness.

Simeon leaves no doubt that, faced with Jesus Christ, all men have to make their decision: those who refuse to accept him as the Saviour, bringing the resurrection to life, prepare their own downfall. The greatest pain for Jesus will be to see that some oppose themselves and refuse salvation. This also is the sharpest sword that wounds the heart of Mary since, with Jesus, her Son and the Son of God, she is mother of all the living, consequently desiring nothing more than the salvation of all.

Heavenly Father, together with Mary and Joseph,
Elizabeth and Zechariah, John the Baptist, Simeon
    and Anna,
we praise you for having sent us Jesus the Prophet.
We praise you for the outpouring of the prophetic
    spirit,
guiding your people in the hours of darkness.
We thank you for all the prophets
who have prepared the coming of Jesus, the Prophet.
Open our eyes, ears and hearts
that we may see salvation
and listen to the voice of the Prophet, Jesus Christ,
as well as to those prophets whom you send in our time,

to shake us, so that we may turn to Jesus
and to you
with all our hearts.

We honour you, Mary, as Queen of the prophets.
Pray for us
that we may always be open to the grace of the
    Holy Spirit
and to the voice of those whose call is to total
    conversion. Amen.

XX

EPIPHANY

'Jesus was born at Bethlehem in Judea during the reign of Herod. After his birth, astrologers from the East arrived in Jerusalem asking, "Where is the child who is born to be king of the Jews? We observed the rising of his star and we have come to pay him homage. King Herod was greatly perturbed when he heard this; and so was the whole of Jerusalem. He called a meeting of the chief priests and lawyers of the Jewish people and put before them the question: "Where is it that the Messiah is to be born?" "At Bethlehem in Judea", they replied; and they referred him to the prophecy which reads: "Bethlehem in the land of Judah, you are far from the least in the eyes of the rulers of Judah; for out of you shall come a leader to be the shepherd of my people Israel".

'Then Herod called the astrologers to meet him in private, and ascertained from them the time when the star had appeared. He sent them on to Bethlehem and said, "Go and make a careful inquiry for the child. When you have found him, report to me so that I may go myself and pay him homage".

'They set out at the king's bidding; and the star which they had seen at its rising went ahead of them until it stopped above the place where the child lay. At the sight of the star, they were overjoyed. Entering the house, they saw the child with Mary, his mother, and bowed to the ground to him; then they opened their treasures and offered him gifts, gold, frankincense and myrrh, and being warned in a dream not to go back to Herod, they returned home another way' (Mt 2:1-12).

This narrative is much more than the account of an event. It is a profound vision of Jesus, the light of all nations, the centre and summit of all history. All the truly religious men of all ages rejoice in his coming. And, if the joy of these men who represent all the godly is so great, how great then must be Mary's joy when realizing the first fulfilment of the prophecy of Simeon: that her Son is to be the Light of all nations. Again we see the relatedness of Mary to the evangelization of all the world. We cannot truly venerate her without an ardent zeal for the salvation of all, so that they may know and praise his name.

'They saw the child with Mary his mother'. The proclamation of all that God has done for Mary and the right veneration of her can do much to prepare the way for faith in Jesus. Not long ago, a concrete experience strengthened this conviction in me. Every Saturday, in Singapore, a city in Asia having a small minority of Christians, twenty thousand persons come to a novena to our Lady of Perpetual Help, where the basic truths of our faith are preached in order that all may find Jesus with Mary his mother. The majority of participants are non-Christian, and each year many hundreds enter the life of the Church, while others continue to pray to Mary and to meditate constantly upon the gospel of Christ.

The event which we celebrate at Epiphany, according to the narrative of Matthew, is rejoicing in the fulfilment of the prophecy of Isaiah: 'You shall see and be radiant, your heart shall thrill and rejoice, because the abundance of the sea shall be turned to you, the wealth of the nations shall come to you. A multitude of camels shall cover you; all those from Sheba shall come. They shall bring gold and frankincense, and shall proclaim the praise of the Lord' (Is 60: 5-6).

The coming of Christ reaches out to all ages and to all people of goodwill. Mary rejoices in all who are given to Jesus in the purity of their heart symbolized by the gold. The purity of motives with which so many seek and find the Lord is related to the immaculate heart of Mary who serves God with the purity of her entire being. Her heart is overflowing with joy when she sees the multitude who seek and find her Son, Jesus, because of the purity of their motives.

The wise men offer frankincense, the symbol of adoration. Mary leads all those who praise the Lord and adore him in all their lives. If we come to Mary, we can learn from her how to follow Christ as true adorers of the Father. When Jesus, later in his ministry, speaks to the woman of Samaria, of the great mystery that God wants adorers 'in spirit and truth', he surely remembers the example of his own mother.

The wise men who seek and find the Lord, offer myrrh which reminds us of the death and sepulchre of Christ. When, later, Mary of Bethany, the sister of Lazarus, will anoint the feet of Jesus with a pound of a very costly perfume, Jesus will explain the meaning of what she does: 'Let her keep it until the day when she prepares for my burial' (Jn 12:7). Mary, the mother of Jesus, is closest to Jesus under the Cross and at the sepulchre of his body given up for us. Her presence is the final test of her adoration of God in the truth and fullness which comes from the Holy Spirit.

We praise you, Father Almighty,
for having sent your Christ to all nations.
Make us grateful for the gift of faith,
that we may all become a living gospel for those
    whom we meet.
Send workers into your vineyard.
Awaken in your Church a new zeal to bring the
    good news to all,
that all may rejoice in Christ
and unite themselves with him,
who, in his humanity, is the perfect adorer of your name.
Cleanse our heart, our intentions,

that we may be able to offer you all that we think,
    desire and do
as a pure sacrifice united with Christ.
May your Holy Spirit teach us how to praise your name,
and how to find the meaning of frustration and
    suffering,
in order to bring it home into the one Eucharist
    offered by Christ.

O Mary, you have offered yourself to God as pure gold.
Seeing your joy at the Epiphany, we ask you to
    pray for us,
that we might consider it the greatest privilege
to be sent as messengers of the good news,
and to preach the gospel, whatever may be the
    cost. Amen.

XXI

THE FLIGHT INTO EGYPT

'An angel of the Lord appeared to Joseph in a dream and said to him, "Rise up and take the child and his mother and escape with them to Egypt and stay there until I tell you, for Herod is going to search for the child to do away with him". So Joseph rose from sleep, and taking the mother and child by night, he went away with them to Egypt, and there he stayed until Herod's death. This was to fulfil what the Lord had declared to the prophet: "I called my Son out of Egypt".

'When Herod saw how the astrologers had tricked him, he fell into a passion and gave orders for the massacre of all the children in Bethlehem and its neighbourhood of the age of two years or less, corresponding with the time he had ascertained from the astrologers. So the words spoken through Jeremiah, the prophet, were fulfilled: "A voice was heard in Rama, wailing and loud laments; it was Rachel weeping for her children and refusing all consolation because they were no more"' (Mt 2:13-18).

When Mary and Joseph have to escape into Egypt to save the life of the child in the land of exile, the prophecy of Simeon comes true. The innocent one, the holy one, becomes a sign of contradiction. While people come from far to seek him, to rejoice in his presence and offer themselves to his service, Herod, the king of Judea, tries to kill him and becomes, indeed, the murderer of many children.

A special divine providence protects the child and his mother, and Joseph is chosen to be the visible sign of this protection.

The Holy Family relives the history of salvation which

is a history of exodus and liberation. Joseph, the patriarch, was sold by his brothers and brought as a slave to Egypt to become the saviour of his brothers. The patriarch Jacob had to go to Egypt, and Moses and the people suffered there under fierce oppression until the Lord freed them from the land of slavery.

Through the prophet Hosea, God calls his people, 'my son', for in the liberation of Israel God acts as Father. 'When Israel was a child, I loved him, and out of Egypt I called my son' (Hos 11:1). All this comes to full truth in Jesus, who with Joseph and his mother has to escape to Egypt and experience this saving action of the Father. He is the beloved Son, and yet he suffers with the down-trodden, with the homeless, and the persecuted.

During our lifetime, we have seen millions of people in various parts of the world driven out of their father-land. Millions of others are migrants looking for work and a piece of bread. No book can contain all the misery and humiliation endured by them. May they remember the experience of Joseph and Mary and Jesus in Egypt. May they turn to Mary in their need, and experience the love of the heavenly Father. If Jesus has taken upon himself this painful exodus, others should not consider it meaningless. And yet we honour the Holy Family who escaped into Egypt, only if we sympathize with the homeless, with the millions of people who live in camps or have to hide their identities because no one wants them.

Scripture does not tell us that Mary came to know about the massacre in Bethlehem, but the thought of such a possibility must have been with Mary and Joseph during the time they spent in Egypt. When they returned to the land of Galilee, they heard about this and about other crimes of Herod; how great must have been her com-passion and the suffering of her immaculate heart. Indeed the prophecy of Simeon stayed with her always.

All-holy God, your ways are wonderful;
your wisdom is above all our human thoughts.

We thank you that through the suffering of Jesus,
    of Mary and Joseph in the land of exile,
you have brought redemption for the terrible suffering
of those who are persecuted, downtrodden and
        homeless.
We pray for them,
that they may not suffer in vain and that their cry
    may be heard.

O Mary, we pray to you, the Mother of Perpetual Help.
May all believers learn from your generosity;
may the rulers of the countries honour God, the
    One Father,
by a greater concern for those who are rejected,
    lonely and homeless.
Pray for us that we may learn compassion,
and unite our actions in the service of those who are
    most in need. Amen.

XXII

IN NAZARETH AND IN THE TEMPLE

'They returned to Galilee to their own town of Nazareth. The child grew big and strong and full of wisdom; and God's favour was with him' (Lk 2:39-40).

God guided Joseph and Mary to bring the child from the land of exile to Galilee, the most humble part of Israel. There, in the house of prayer in Nazareth, Jesus grows up. The evangelist underlines the true humanity of Jesus. Like other children, Jesus grows up, but unlike others, he is already full of wisdom and radiant in the grace of God. Mary helps the growth of Jesus in consciousness, in the capacity to walk, to talk, to respond and to manifest the usual signs of love, the creative freedom of Jesus. In this period of growth, Mary, doubtless, plays a privileged role. Like a pure mirror, she reflects the divine love; it is she, with Joseph, who sings the songs of the Servant and her life is the best commentary on them. As Jesus grows each day, she can better understand this wonderful prophecy. It is her blessedness to see the graciousness of Jesus, the spontaneity of his prayer-life, the graciousness in helping others.

'Now it was the practice of his parents to go to Jerusalem every year for the feast of the Passover; and when Jesus was twelve, they made the pilgrimage as usual. When the festive season was over and they started for home, the boy Jesus stayed behind in Jerusalem. His parents did not know of this; but thinking that he was with the party, they journeyed on for a whole day, and only then did they begin looking for him among their friends and relations. As they could not find him, they returned to Jerusalem to look for him; and after three days, they found him sitting in the temple, surrounded by the teachers, listening to them and putting questions; and all who heard him were amazed at his intelligence and the answers he gave. His parents were astonished to see him there, and his mother said to him, "My son, why have you treated us like this? Your father and I have been searching for you in great anxiety?" "What made you search?" he said, "Did you not know that I was bound to be in my Father's house?" But they did not understand what he meant. Then he went back with them to Nazareth, and continued to be under their authority; his mother treasured up all these things in her heart. As Jesus grew up, he advanced in wisdom and in favour with God and men' (Lk 2:41-52).

The episode in the temple is a great prophecy: the detachment of Christ, the pilgrim, from his family is beginning. It entails shock and great anxiety. Up to that point, Mary and Joseph had known Jesus in a gracious dependence on them and attention to them. He evidently had never undertaken anything without the knowledge of his parents. And now, suddenly, he makes visible his mission, which entails suffering and the profound experience of the exodus for Mary. The event foreshadows the time when Jesus will leave his home in Nazareth to spend forty days in the desert, and later to become a pilgrim as the living gospel in Galilee and Judea. The prophecy goes even beyond that detachment: there are three days filled with anguish; they announce the three days between the death of Jesus on the cross and his resurrection.

This biblical text is of paramount importance. The first time we hear Jesus call the Almighty God, 'Father', (and it is no longer just a general expression), he says, 'My Father'. It is the profound expression of the relationship between Jesus and the One who sent him. It is the word that engraves itself more than any other on the memory of the Church throughout the centuries.

This word of Jesus spoken in the temple after his surprising detachment from Mary and Joseph, indicates the new family, the whole family of the redeemed that is based upon the unique relationship of Jesus of Nazareth to the Fatherhood of God. This word, *'Abba*, Father', is to be the last word that Jesus speaks on the cross. Each Israelite ends his day with a prayer to Yahweh: 'Into thy hands, I entrust my spirit'. The unheard of newness, however, is that on the cross, Jesus adds this word, 'Father'. He has manifested him as the Father of all. Totally new horizons open up in the history of salvation, and the risen Lord speaking to Mary Magdalen makes clear the dimensions of the new family, 'my Father and your Father'. Before his ascension, he will promise the Holy Spirit, referring again to that unique name of Father: 'I am sending upon you my Father's promised gift. So stay here in this city until you are armed with power from above' (Lk 24:49).

The coming of the Holy Spirit upon the apostles gathered around Mary will give life to the new family promised by the prophetic event in the temple when the twelve-year-old Jesus reveals his relationship to the Almighty for the first time. The new family of God will manifest itself everywhere throughout history where people are moved by the Spirit of God and recognize themselves as sons and daughters of God. 'The Spirit makes us children enabling us to cry, *"Abba,* Father!"' (Rom 8:14-15).

Mary, the mother of Jesus of Nazareth, is called to enter into a new dimension of consciousness. Her role is even greater: she is to be the mother of the Church; she has a motherhood in the new family of God based on the relationship of Jesus to his heavenly Father and the Holy Spirit. Mary, strong in faith and filled with motherly love, lives in the nearness of Jesus; but she is also to undergo the dark night of faith. In spite of her absolute purity and docility, she is not able at once to understand the full depth of the events nor the words of Jesus. However, all that she is, does and says, is a prayer that Jesus may reveal to her the mystery, and the meaning of the words he speaks in this event. She treasures up his words in her heart until she comes to the full understanding of them.

In the lives of Jesus and Mary, there is no place for what we call 'conversion'. In them, there is no shadow of sin, but they too live under the law of growth. It is remarkable that Luke, in one and the same chapter, twice emphasizes that Jesus advanced in wisdom and in favour with God and man. This is important too for the Church, in her gradual grasping of her mission and in the on-going effort of deciphering the signs of the times.

We thank you, Father, Father of our Lord Jesus Christ,
    and our Father,
that in the temple you have manifested the wisdom
    of your Son, Jesus.
We shall never be able to thank you enough
for the glad news that there is, among us, a Brother
who can call you with full right, 'My Father',
and who entitles us to join him in the new family
and to call you, 'Our Father'.
Lord God, our Father,
make us holy, make us one in your love.

We thank you, O Mary,
for your motherly care for Jesus our Brother and
    our Lord.
We are deeply touched by the pain and anguish of
    your heart
in that prophetic event foreshadowing three even more
    anguishing days
after the death of your Son, Jesus Christ.
Pray for us
that we may treasure up the words of Jesus in our hearts
as you did,
and that we may be patient and faithful in our
    common effort
to reach a deeper understanding of the words of Jesus
and a fuller discernment of the signs of the times. Amen.

XXIII

MARY'S ROLE IN THE FIRST MIRACLE

'There was a wedding at Cana in Galilee. The mother of Jesus was there, and Jesus and his disciples were guests also. The wine gave out; so Jesus' mother said to him, "They have no wine left". He answered: "O woman, what does this mean for you and me? My hour has not yet come". His mother said to the servants, "Do whatever he tells you". There were six stone water jars standing near, of the kind used for Jewish rites of purification; each held from twenty to thirty gallons. Jesus said to the servants, "Fill the jars with water", and they filled them to the brim. "Now draw some off", he ordered, "and take it to the steward of the feast", and they did so. The steward tasted the water now turned into wine, not knowing its source, though the servants who had drawn the water knew. He hailed the bridegroom and said, "Everyone serves the best wine first and waits until the guests have drunk freely before serving the poorer sort; but you have kept the best wine until now". This deed at Cana in Galilee is the first of the signs by which Jesus revealed his glory and led his disciples to believe in him' (Jn 2:1-11).

This narrative brings the image of Mary down to earth and exalts her to heaven. It is, at the same time, a manifestation of Mary's loving attention to the earthly needs of people and her prophetic intuition of an event that goes far beyond daily life. As in the house of Zechariah, so we find her again in Cana as a humble servant who helps out in the household. It is probably a gesture of courtesy towards Mary that Jesus and his disciples are invited. The fact that he comes with quite a number of friends

F

might partially be the cause of the embarrassment, that, in the end, there is no wine. That she brings the matter before her son is an expression of both her goodness and her inspiration by the Holy Spirit. She does not tell Jesus what to do. Her prayer is courageous and at the same time humble. This is a model for our prayer. Are we not sometimes tempted to tell God what he should do instead of simply opening our needs before him and asking him for the grace that our wills may be totally conformed to his will? In a humble prayer like that of Mary, we begin to discover dimensions far beyond immediate needs, and we come to realize that the Lord always knows better what is truly good for us.

Jesus' miracle at Cana as a response to his mother is a prophetic event. Each word and action is rich in meaning and opens up new horizons. The word of Mary to the servants, a word that seems directed to each of us, deserves our special attention: 'Do whatever he tells you'. This is at the heart of true Marian devotion. Mary, our mother, has no greater desire than to draw all our attention, love and obedience to Jesus. We honour her as we follow him and do whatever he tells us by his word, grace, life and death as well as all the events of his life.

The prayer of Mary is the occasion of the first great sign in which Jesus reveals his divine power. She is like the friend of an artist who sometimes, through a humble suggestion, brings the artist to full intuition in his work. The first response of Jesus finds various translations, but the words must be seen in their context. They contain no refusal or blame.

Jesus, on this occasion, does not say, 'mother', but rather, 'woman'. It is the same expression as in the great promise of God in the proto-evangelium: 'I will put enmity between you and the woman' (Gen 3:15). On the Cross, Jesus again addresses his mother as 'woman'; and the vision of the great woman initiated by the book of Genesis comes to its full magnitude in the book of Revelation, chapter twelve. In the eyes of Jesus, in that solemn moment in Cana, Mary is more than his private mother. She is the great sign of promise, a prophetic sign affirmed by the first miracle which Jesus works in view of her, the 'woman'.

Jesus says, 'My hour has not yet come'. The present event, as great as it is, has to be read in the light of the great hour of Jesus when he is to shed the blood of the new and eternal covenant, wedding himself forever with redeemed humanity. Christ is the bridegroom who preserves the best wine until the end.

The embarrassment of the bride and bridegroom of Cana, which gives rise to such a great miracle, is a modest symbol of the profound suffering in which the wedding between Christ and the Church is prepared. Mary is present at both events. She will always invite and urge us: 'Do whatever he tells you'. And, her words are both an exhortation and a gift.

We praise you, Father of our Lord Jesus Christ;
for in this event, you have revealed the new Adam,
and the new Eve, the immaculate woman,
the proto-type of the Church.
We thank you; for by your Spirit you have inspired the
    humble prayer
which gives rise to the first sign of our salvation.
Grant to us your grace,
that in this event and in all events of our lives
we may discover the profound meaning of salvation.

O Mary, how beautiful is your trusting prayer!
You know how to honour Jesus by your prayer.
Pray for us that we, like you at Cana,
may learn to intercede for one another,
while ready to help one another
and bear one another's burdens. Amen.

XXIV

NAZARETH REJECTS THE SON OF MARY

'Hear, O heavens, and give ear, O earth; for the Lord has spoken: "Sons have I reared and brought up, but they have rebelled against me. The ox knows its owner, and the ass its master's grip; but Israel does not know. My people does not understand"' (Is 1:2-3).

The heart of the prophet Isaiah must have been pierced when the Lord bade him announce this terrible suffering of God's own heart. How must have been pierced then the heart of Mary, when she experienced the concreteness of this prophecy in her own town of Nazareth. The gospel of St Luke gives us a live description.

'Then Jesus, armed with the power of the Spirit, returned to Galilee; and reports about him spread through the whole countryside. He taught in their synagogues and all men sang his praises.

So he came to Nazareth, where he had been brought up, and went to the synagogue on the sabbath day as he regularly did. He stood up to read the lesson, and was handed the scroll of the prophet Isaiah. He opened the scroll and found the passage which says,

"The Spirit of the Lord is upon me because he has anointed me;
he has sent me to announce good news to the poor,
to proclaim release for prisoners and recovery of sight for the blind;
to let broken victims go free,
to proclaim the year of the Lord's favour".

He rolled up the scroll, gave it back to the attendant, and sat down; and all eyes in the synagogue were fixed on him. He began to speak: "Today", he said, "in your hearing, this text has come true!" There was a general stir of admiration; they were surprised that words of such grace should fall from his lips. "Is not this Joseph's son?" they asked. Then Jesus said, "No doubt you will quote to me the proverb, 'Physician, heal yourself', and say, 'We have heard of all your doings at Capernaum; do the same here in your own town'". "I tell you this", he went on, "No prophet is recognized in his own country. There were many widows in Israel, you may be sure, in Elijah's time, when for three years and six months the skies never opened, and famine lay hard over the whole country; yet it was to none of those that Elijah was sent, but to a widow at Sarepta in the territory of Sidon. Again, in the time of the prophet Elisha, there were many lepers in Israel, and not one of them was healed, but only Naaman the Syrian". At these words, the whole congregation was infuriated. They leapt up, threw him out of the town and took him to the brow of the hill on which it was built, meaning to hurl him over the edge. But he walked straight through them all and went away' (Lk 4:14-30).

This passage of great relevance is similar in story to Matthew 13:53-58 and Mark 6:1-6, where the people refer explicitly to Mary: 'Is not this the carpenter, the son of Mary?' The mother of Jesus was most probably present at these happenings. Jesus was deeply hurt: 'He was taken aback by their want of faith' (Mk 6:6). How great must have been the hurt in Mary's heart.

We cannot avoid asking the question: Why was Jesus rejected by his own townsfolk? The answer seems to be that Jesus came from humble people. Everyone knew his mother Mary and his parents; all of them were of humble social condition. In full line with this, Jesus presents himself explicitly as the Servant of God and man. Thus, Jesus, by his very origin at the human level, by his life-style and by his words, thoroughly rejects the false messianic expectations. So many had anticipated a national hero, and the gospel text indicates that his own people wanted him to be a miracle worker for their own greater glory. They were jealous because he had made his home in Capernaum, and there manifested great signs. Thus the townspeople felt that he was sinning against their collective interests.

In the conduct of the people of Nazareth is symbolically expressed the sin of a great part of Israel. The high priests, the pharisees, the powerful, used religion as a means, and had Jesus allowed himself to be used for their self-interest, he would have served their false purposes and have violated his true mission as the Servant of Yahweh. Because he refused to play into the hands of such people, Jesus was rejected and scorned. No one else could so profoundly have understood this conflict between the Servant of God and the false messianic expectation as Mary, the humble handmaid of God. This sad event in Nazareth was, for Mary, a prophecy of what might happen at the end.

We see Mary, the mother of Jesus and our mother, as one who suffered in this moment and throughout the months to come, for all the sins of humankind, for all the collective egotism, arrogance and pride which lead to the rejection of Christ the Servant. All this serves as a motive to venerate Mary, who teaches us how to follow Jesus in humility and detachment, sharing in Christ's suffering. Honouring Mary means never using the Church for personal gain, prestige, wealth, power or title, but rather, honouring the Church as humble servants of Christ.

Almighty and all-merciful God, help your people,
that all may come to know the name of Jesus,
    'Servant of God'.
Protect your Church that, with Mary, the humble
    handmaid,
she may always be a sign of Christ the Saviour.
Open the eyes of those who wrongly seek honour
    and favours

instead of following Christ,
crucified for us.

O Mary, we honour your suffering,
your pain caused by those whom you loved.
How deep must have been the wound in your heart
when you saw Jesus rejected by your neighbours!
We are all written into your heart,
and we should know how deeply we wound your heart,
when we refuse to accept Christ as the Servant,
and follow him in humility as you did.
Pray for us
that we may come to accept all the frustrations
      and sufferings
with which the Lord allows us to be afflicted
on this road of salvation,
and thus come to know more intensely Christ,
the Suffering Servant,
and you, his mother, who followed him on his road.
      Amen.

XXV

THE TRUE FAMILY OF JESUS

'Jesus entered a house; and once more such a crowd collected round them that they had no chance to eat. When his family heard of this, they set out to take charge of him; "He is out of his mind", they said.

'The doctors of the law, too, who had come from Jerusalem, said, "He is possessed by Beelzebub", and "He drives out devils by the prince of devils". He called them to come forward and spoke to them in parables. "How can Satan drive out Satan? If a kingdom is divided against itself, that kingdom cannot stand; and if Satan is in rebellion against himself, he is divided and cannot stand; and that is the end of him. On the other hand, no one can break into a strong man's house and make off with his goods unless he has first tied the strong man up; then he can ransack the house. I tell you this: no sin, no slander is beyond forgiveness for man, but whoever slanders the Holy Spirit can never be forgiven; he is guilty of eternal sin". He said this because they had declared that he was possessed by an unclean spirit.

'Then his mother and his brothers arrived, and remaining outside, sent in a message asking him to come out to them. A crowd was sitting round as word was brought to him: "Your mother and your brothers are outside asking for you". He replied, "Who is my mother? Who are my brothers?" And looking round at those who were sitting in the circle about him, he said, "Here are my mother and my brothers. Whoever does the will of God is my brother, my sister, my mother" ' (Mk 3:20-35).

This narrative may be surprising to those who have a

tender devotion to Mary, but it would be erroneous to think that Mary, the mother of Jesus, was among those who said, 'He is out of his mind'. She surely was not one desirous of restraining Jesus. Mary is a believer, not a manipulator. In fact, Mary's suffering must have been great, seeing the lack of faith and reverence towards her Son of the members of her own family. It seems that she was most painfully caught up in their manoeuvre. Probably she was there in order to quiet them and to bring them to a proper frame of mind.

The words of Jesus are, on the one hand, a detachment from his natural family, and even from his mother as far as physical motherhood is concerned. They are the expression of the same detachment or exodus which we have seen in the narrative about Jesus in the temple. ' "What made you search?", he said. "Did you not know that I was bound to be in my Father's house?" ' Now it became even clearer that Jesus had not come to build up his own little family, but rather, to give existence to the world-wide family of disciples, a family based entirely upon the universal fatherhood of almighty God, his Father, and upon his own being as the Brother of all. In this perspective, then, we can understand the situation from our own families, particularly when they try to obstruct our total adherence to the kingdom of God. Let us never forget, too, that the detachment is only one aspect. It is part of the wonderful expression of the good news that those who follow Christ whole-heartedly, whatever may be the price, are as dear to him as brothers and sisters are. Moreover, they are as dear to him as his mother. This expression of our Master's love for us leads us then to a better understanding of a similar and even more profound expression: 'As the Father has loved me, so I have loved you' (Jn 15:9).

Mary, totally consecrated to the kingdom of the Father and to the mission of the Servant of God, is never an obstacle to the mission of Christ. On the contrary, her entire life helps us to understand the meaning of detachment, of exodus, as she follows Christ in his most crucial moments, particularly in this humiliating circumstance, and more so when she stands beneath the Cross. If we are ready to follow Mary along this road, then perhaps in moments of deepest suffering we shall understand more fully what it means to be as dear to Jesus as his mother; we shall hear and understand the word: 'Son, see your mother'.

Thus we can realize that this response of Jesus to those who did not yet know that he was the cornerstone of a new universal family does not at all estrange us from Mary, but helps us to understand her role in the new family of God. And we know that she will be present with us in the moments of greatest temptation in our life if only we are ready to follow the Servant of God.

We praise you, Father of our Lord Jesus,
that in your beloved Son you have given us the
    privilege
of belonging to your family
and of calling you, with Jesus, Father.
We thank you, Jesus, for your infinite love,
that is as tender as the love of a mother
and even more tender than that of the greatest mother,
    your own.
If we join you in love for your mother
and come to realize more completely how tenderly
    you loved her,
we can come closer to you and understand more deeply
how much you love us when, like Mary, we listen to
    your word,
treasure it up in our heart,
ready to put it into practice.
Grant to us, O Lord,
the ability to be true listeners to your word,
able to respond with all our hearts in all our lives.

O Mary, in the midst of the pain
caused by members of your family,

you have rejoiced,
hearing that your Son loves all of us, your children,
with the same love with which he loves you.
Knowing this, we also know how great your love is
    for us
when we put all our trust in Jesus.
Pray for us, O Mary, that we may be grateful for
    this privilege,
and that nothing in this world may hinder us from
    following Christ
wholeheartedly
as a member of the new family which honours the
    one Father in heaven,
and pays tribute also to you, the mother of the living.
    Amen.

XXVI

WITH MARY, HEARERS OF THE WORD

'While he was speaking thus, a woman in the crowd called out, "Happy the womb that carried you and the breasts that suckled you!" He answered, "Happy rather are those who hear the word of God and keep it" ' (Lk 11:27-28).

Jesus had driven out a devil and had healed the dumb man so that he could speak and praise the Lord. Those in high positions in the Jewish Church had just scorned Jesus, whereas the contrasting figure is the humble woman in the crowd who, with great admiration and faith, praises Jesus in praising his mother. Jesus accepts this beautiful expression of human sentiment but, as always, deepens the understanding of it. Not wanting to diminish the glory of his mother — on the contrary, he emphasizes the one dimension that is the true glory of Mary, the mother in the new family of God, as one whose openness to the word of God is dedication to living the truth.

This is consistent with the whole intention of the gospel of St Luke who repeatedly shows Mary as the model of faith. He makes this clear from the moment of the Incarnation ('Behold, here I am, the servant of the Lord'), in the Visitation ('Happy is she who has had faith that the Lord's promise would be fulfilled'), in her silent and yet eloquent response to the song of the angels and the message of the shepherds ('Mary treasured up all these things and pondered over them'), and again as the last word, to the event in the temple when Jesus shows his detachment from his natural family ('His mother treasured up all these things in her heart').

In the sermon on the mount, Jesus teaches most solemnly the distinctive characteristic of his new family: it is not sufficient to call oneself his disciple; what is needed is openness to his word in the sense of listening and in the sense of responding. 'Not everyone who calls me "Lord, Lord" will enter the kingdom of heaven, but only those who do the will of my heavenly Father. The one who hears these words of mine and acts on them is like a man who had the sense to build his house on rock' (Mt 7:21-24).

Thus, Jesus reveals to us the true motherhood of Mary as the prototype of the Church, who lives by every word that comes from the mouth of God and is totally dedicated to act upon that word.

The future of Christianity depends greatly upon each community's knowing how to celebrate the Eucharist, the memorial of our Lord's suffering, death and resurrection, which means also having the readiness to live according to this mystery. We can be sure of Mary's intercession if we are willing to learn from her and to follow her example. She is the perfect Eucharistic person, the model of grateful memory, who guarantees fidelity in our commitment to the kingdom of God.

If we want to be authentic members of the new family grounded in faith in Christ, then we have to learn more deeply the art of discovering the signs of God's presence, of listening to his word: in all of creation; in the human person, as image and likeness of God; in the saints and the prophets; and in the wonderful message of the sacraments — always relying on the grace of the Holy Spirit to help us decipher the message and the will of God. With Mary the Virgin, we shall daily meditate upon the scriptures; we shall also give full attention to the magisterium of the Church in order better to understand the total message of Christ. However, the heart of the matter is always what Mary teaches us: 'Do whatever he tells you'.

Glory and praise to you, all-holy God;
for through all your works you speak to us.
Everything directs our attention to your only-begotten
    Son
who is your final word to us,
the full revelation of your love and your will.
Send us your Holy Spirit that we may always listen
    to your word
with a pure heart,
and with a firm purpose to act accordingly.

O Mary, pray for us
that the Lord may give us, as he gave you,
a grateful memory,
so that each day we may learn best how to celebrate
    the Eucharist
and to live our life in grateful response
to all of God's gifts. Amen.

XXVII

THE SORROWFUL MOTHER

'Near the cross where Jesus hung, stood his mother' (Jn 19:25).

We have accompanied Mary on the various stations of her exodus, of her detachment and pilgrimage. We have seen her when, with child, she had to leave home and give birth to Jesus as the poorest of all pilgrims. When the prophet Simeon announces to Mary that a sword would pierce her heart, she is already acquainted with that thought. Crossing the desert with Joseph and the child and coming to live as a migrant in Egypt, thus recalling the history of her people, Mary anticipates in her own experience the final rejection of Jesus by his own people. The three days of anguish in seeking and finally finding Jesus in the temple foretell future anxiety. No one suffers as deeply as his mother when Jesus does not find faith among those whom God has especially prepared by his revelation.

Mary is not present at the triumphant entry of Jesus into Jerusalem, but she is present at the decisive hour of the redemption of the world, under the Cross. More than a mother suffers at childbirth, Mary suffers hearing the words of anguish from Jesus, 'My God, my God, why hast thou forsaken me?' She is no less shaken in heart than Jesus is, and is also one with him when he entrusts himself totally into the hands of his Father. During the passion and death of Jesus, Mary lives the pain and the blessedness that no one can understand so well as Jesus himself: 'Blessed are the sorrowful for they will be comforted'. With Jesus, she suffers in redemptive compassion. Her sorrow is an expression of faith and love. It is a sign of her role in the new family in which everyone knows the law of Christ, that is, to bear the burdens of one another. United with Christ, Mary bears our burden.

Mary knows the name of Jesus, 'The Covenant of the People'; she lives the mystery of saving solidarity of which the apostle of the Gentiles will speak so convincingly: 'It is now my happiness to suffer for you. This is my way of helping to complete, in my poor flesh, the full tale of Christ's affliction still to be endured, for the sake of his body which is the Church' (Col 1:24). Mary the servant of salvation has lived this mystery in an outstanding way as the new Eve totally associated with the new Adam. It is not that Jesus' suffering would not be complete without Mary's sufferings. On the contrary, it is the overflowing power of Christ's death and resurrection that gives first to Mary and then to all the disciples of Christ, the power to share in his saving solidarity.

When we call Mary the new Eve, or the 'Co-redemptrix' or servant of salvation, this does not mean in any way to deny that Christ alone is the Mediator, our Saviour, our Redeemer, but it expresses the super-abundance that is in Christ's suffering, death and resurrection, and it is a praise and thanksgiving offered to our Mediator and Redeemer, who allows us to be humble sharers in his work. So we can, with Paul, offer thanksgiving even for our frustrations and sufferings; it is not thanksgiving for suffering as such, but for the transfiguration of suffering and death in the saving solidarity with the death and resurrection of Christ. Our share cannot be understood without paying full attention to the privileged share of the new Eve, Mary.

A personal experience helped me and may help others to understand this great mystery of sharing in Christ's redeeming sufferings. More than twenty years ago, I paid a visit to a famous Protestant theologian who had once been a Catholic priest and teacher of dogmatic theology. Because of the issue of celibacy, he had left not only the priesthood, but also his Church. He was already ill when I went to see him. With a gesture of welcome, he said, 'After forty years, you are the first priest to visit me'. We had a long and very good talk; it became clear to me that in his heart he still belonged to the Catholic Church. But how could I hope that he would have the courage to take the step he somehow desired, having been a famous man in his Church? I wrote to a former companion of his, Joseph Bernhardt, who in the era of modernism and anti-modernism, had had difficulty with the Church, married, but then was reconciled, and in Hitler's time had been one of the most courageous witnesses to faith. I asked him whether he would be ready to visit his former friend and listen to the desires of his heart. He did, and wrote to me: 'I had the same impression; his conscience does not yet seem to be settled, but only the prayer and sacrifice of a saint can obtain such a great grace'. I spoke about this matter to one of my penitents whom I considered a saint. I did not ask her anything, knowing that she would join us in our prayers. But she did more; spontaneously, she offered her life, if such an offer could bring the needed grace to this man who, I told her, had always remained faithful to devotion to Mary. She fell into a deadly illness, suffering great pain, but refused any medication. Before her death, she expressed her firm trust that the Lord had heard her prayers. She died on Epiphany. The following day, the former priest, who had been put into hospital, asked suddenly of the young physician attending him: 'What would the world say if after all, I should return to the Catholic Church?' The inspired response was another question: 'Dear Professor, in a few weeks, you will have only one question: "What did God say?" ' In a quick decision, he urged the physician to call the priest immediately. He made his confession and called his wife to declare his intention to die as a member of the Catholic Church.

Whatever may be our active share in the mystery of redemption, it is always the harvest of the passion, death

99

and resurrection of our Lord Jesus Christ. And we shall never forget the special share which Mary has had and continues to have in this great mystery.

> We praise you, all-holy and all-merciful Father,
> for the passion, death and resurrection of Jesus,
>   your Son,
> that transformed the meaning of our suffering and
>   our death.
> We are redeemed from the slavery of sin
> if we gratefully and actively enter into the mystery
>   of redemption.
> We praise you for the mission you have entrusted
>   to Mary,
> the new Eve,
> the sorrowful Mother in this mystery.
> Make us grateful and give us the courage to take
>   upon ourselves
> our cross,
> and to bear a part of the burden of our brothers
>   and sisters.

> O sorrowful Mother of Jesus,
> you are blessed,
> for your suffering was not like that of those
> who are caught in the solidarity of sin and the
>   emptiness of a selfish world.
> Yours was a suffering similar to that of Christ.
> You who have suffered with faith, with hope,
> and in love for all of us,
> pray for us that we may, with you,
> follow Christ on the road of the Cross. Amen.

XXVIII

'SEE YOUR MOTHER'

'Jesus saw his mother with the disciple he loved standing beside her. He said to her, "Woman, there is your son"; and to the disciple, "There is your mother"; and from that moment, the disciple took her into his home' (Jn 19:26-27).

Aware that his death was approaching, Jesus, as the head of a small family, takes care of his mother, entrusting her to his best and most faithful friend, the virginal disciple, John. What every thoughtful man does on his deathbed, Christ does on the altar of the Cross, and he does it with unique tenderness. His words and his gestures have, however, a much broader sense; this is even indicated by the careful wording of the text. The gospel of John says that Jesus saw 'his mother'. Then when Jesus addresses her, he calls her 'woman'. He addressed her not only as his mother, but as that 'woman' of which the proto-evangelium in Genesis, chapter three, speaks. We see this prophetic meaning in the word 'woman' early, when Mary played a providential role in the first miracle of Jesus. Not only entrusting his mother to John but inviting John to see his mother in the 'woman' predicted in the book of Genesis, Jesus makes clear that he now speaks on the level of the new family of which he, the new Adam, is the head, and in which his mother, the new Eve, has a unique role.

We are invited by the very testament of Jesus to venerate her spiritual motherhood. Honouring this role and mission of Mary, proclaimed at the moment of the great exodus when Jesus gave his life for us on the Cross, we can never forget the detachment entailed as well as the subsequent life of the exodus. Thus, when we are invited with John to look at Mary as our mother, we stand with profound veneration before the new Eve, the mother of the living, the great sign of which the Apocalypse speaks.

We love our mother with the love of Jesus, and we love her gratefully because she has brought us to life in the pangs of childbirth suffered by Christ himself on the Cross and suffered by her also.

The spiritual motherhood of Mary unites us in a special way in the all-embracing solidarity of salvation that has its source, centre and summit in Jesus Christ. We rightly venerate Mary as the Mother of the Church. And we honour her truly when we live as fully as possible the saving event, bearing one another's burdens, praying and suffering that, finally, all may be one in the love of God.

We thank you, heavenly Father, that you have given
   us everything
in Jesus Christ, your only-begotten Son, our Mediator
   and Saviour.
And we thank you that you have given him
Mary as the servant of salvation, the new Eve,
the mother of the living.
And our hearts are filled with gratitude
that you have given her to us in a unique spiritual
   motherhood.
May your Holy Spirit come upon us
that, with Mary, we may live in the solidarity of faith,
   hope and love,
and bear fruit for the life of the world.

O Mary, Mother of God, our mother,
pray for us now and at the hour of our death
that we may always praise your Son Jesus Christ
for his salvation of mankind,
and live the mystery of saving solidarity,
and thus be freed from perdition and the fear of death.
   Amen.

XXIX

MARY'S EASTER JOY AND OURS

'Early on the Sunday morning, while it was still dark, Mary of Magdala came to the tomb. She saw that the stone had been moved away from the entrance, and she ran to Simon Peter and the other disciple, the one whom Jesus loved. "They have taken the Lord out of the tomb", she cried, "and we do not know where they have laid him". So Peter and the other set out and made their way to the tomb. They were running side by side, but the other disciple outran Peter and reached the tomb first. He peered in and saw the linen wrappings lying there, but did not enter. Then Simon Peter came up following him, and he went into the tomb. He saw the linen wrappings lying, and the napkin which had been over his head, not lying with the wrappings but rolled together in a place by itself. Then the disciple who had reached the tomb first went in too, and he saw and believed' (Jn 20: 1-8).

On Easter morning, we find Peter with John, to whom Mary had been entrusted. Did she know it? We might well think that she herself had encouraged the beloved disciple to look for Peter knowing the abyss of his sadness and depression. In the image and likeness of Mary, John, the virginal disciple of Christ, is the man waiting for the coming of the Lord and so he discovers his neighbour's need. He who had taken Mary into his home, shares her maternal care for all, but especially for those who have a special mission in the Church.

I often ask myself how it is possible that the texts of the gospel should speak of the Easter faith of so many others and not that of Mary, the mother of Jesus. The answer might be this: The gospels underline two aspects: first, the faith that Christ is truly risen and that he has revealed himself, and secondly, that the disciples came only gradually to the fullness of faith. Mary, who had fully lived the exodus with her Son, Jesus, who shared the depth of his mystery with him, Mary the most humble of all, did not have the difficulty which Peter, Mary Magdalen and the disciples of Emmaus had in coming to belief in the resurrection. She, our spiritual mother, is the prototype of the Easter faith of the whole Church. Intimately united with the suffering and death of Jesus, she is equally united with the joy of his resurrection. The closer to her we live, the greater will be our Easter joy, and the more fruitful our road to fullness of faith.

The gospel presents us with a number of other women who, even before the apostles, came to faith in Jesus Christ. John, the beloved disciple of Jesus, to whom Mary is entrusted, gives particular attention to the road of faith of Mary Magdalen. She too, in her own way, is a prototype of our faith in so far as our faith needs further purification, greater clarity and strength. Mary Magdalen seeks and finds Jesus because of her great love, although the full light of faith does not break through at once. Both Mary, the mother of Jesus, and Mary Magdalen together, should be present to our meditation: the immaculate faith of maturity on the one hand, and on the other, faith still in need of search and purification.

Easter day is greatly concerned with the role of women. Mary, the queen of the apostles, is *the* woman. She is the one who, with all her being, sings the song of the Servant and the joy of the resurrection. At her side are other women, who in the depth of their faith are, as it were, apostles to the twelve. And we can never forget that at the heart of the Church there are with Mary all those who believe in the risen Lord and spread this faith with all their being.

We thank you, Father, for the gift of faith and the
    Easter joy
which you have given first to Mary, the Mother of Jesus,
then to John, the beloved apostle,
to Mary Magdalen and to many others including
    ourselves.
May we run on the road of faith like John,
and search for you with great love as Mary Magdalen
    did,
and find, with all our hearts and minds, Jesus,
who reveals to us the depth of your love.
Lord, grant us a humble and grateful faith,
full of joy.

O Mary, blessed are you;
for you have believed that God's promise will be
    fulfilled.
Blessed are you in your Easter joy,
rejoicing in the faith of the apostles,
and in the faith of so many humble people.
Pray for us that we seek first of all a living,
    grateful faith,
a faith that bears fruit in love and justice
for the salvation of the world,
a faith that brings all to know Jesus Christ,
the Son of the living God,
whom we have the honour to call your Son. Amen.

XXX

MARY AND PENTECOST

'Then they returned to Jerusalem. Entering the city, they went to the room upstairs where they were lodging: Peter and John and James and Andrew, Philip and Thomas, Bartholomew and Matthew, James the son of Alphaeus and Simon the Zealot and Judas the son of James. All these were constantly at prayer together, and with them a group of women, including Mary the mother of Jesus, and his brothers' (Acts 1:12-14).

Mary, the mother of Jesus, who since the great moment of redemption has become also the mother of John and of all of us, is with the apostles at Pentecost. She lives her role in the new family of God represented by the apostles and the holy women and some of her relatives who followed her in faith. Her prayer and her presence among the apostles is essential for the preparation of the event of Pentecost. Mary, who is full of grace, totally guided by the Spirit, is indispensable for our life of prayer and to the road to faith. The powerful coming of the Holy Spirit is prepared by the prayer and expectation of Mary, and of the whole community with her.

'And they were all filled with the Holy Spirit' (Acts 2:4). The Church was already the Church of paschal faith, but it is the power of the Holy Spirit which gives her full life in a new Pentecost. It becomes clear how central to the Church is Mary's faith: 'We believe in the Holy Spirit, the Giver of Life'. He has spoken through the prophets and in a special way through Mary, the Queen of the prophets. Openness to the Spirit is always a gift of Christ, the new

Adam, and can therefore never be severed from the role of Mary, the new Eve, the mother of the living.

Mary, Virgin and Mother, is the first to experience the power of the Holy Spirit. She has not only conceived the Word Incarnate by the Holy Spirit; she also becomes the model of faith through the grace of the same Holy Spirit. More than all the others, she experienced the joy of Easter as a gift of the Spirit; she is fully at home with the new family of Jesus when they are filled with the Holy Spirit. More even than the apostle, she can exultantly say, 'Thanks be to God . . . for in Christ Jesus, the life-giving law of the Spirit has set us free from the law of sin and death' (Rom 7:25; 8:2).

Mary was never submitted to the law of sin. In God's design, and in her existence from beginning to end, she is living the new solidarity that comes from Christ who is the Covenant of the people. She has no reason to fear death. Death will be for her the final home-coming into the glory of her Son. She lives fully and knows the liberating law of the Spirit that unites her with Jesus who is the Christ, the One anointed by the Holy Spirit.

Mary, more than all the others saved by Jesus Christ, bears the fruit of the Spirit. 'The harvest of the Spirit is love, joy, peace, patience, kindness, goodness, fidelity, gentleness and self-control' (Gal 5:22).

Mary, the Bride of the Holy Spirit, invites the whole Church and each of us constantly to an intense life of prayer, to trust in the Lord, to praise and give thanks, and thus be faithful to the covenant. An authentic devotion to Mary goes hand in hand with a strengthened faith in the Holy Spirit and an increasing docility towards his grace. Whoever loves and venerates Mary and adores the Holy Spirit with her cannot live like a slave under the law. He will be able to live the new law that is manifested in the Eucharist and will consider the gifts of the Holy Spirit together with the needs of his fellowmen as the supreme rule. This belongs to the very essence of the new birth in Christ and the ongoing spiritual renewal of the

Church. We shall never be able to see the hoped-for new Pentecost of the Church of which John XXIII has spoken with so great a trust, unless we nourish a deep love and veneration for Mary who teaches us how the whole Church can become a house of prayer, and how we can all learn to become adorers of God in spirit and truth.

We thank you, heavenly Father, for having given us,
     in Mary,
the model of fidelity to the law of the Spirit,
of glad faith and firm commitment to the messianic
     peace.
May your Holy Spirit come upon us abundantly
and transform us that we too may bear fruit in justice,
in love, joy, peace, goodness and gentleness
for the life of the world.

O Mary, you were the heart of the Church
when the apostles expected
and experienced
the powerful coming of the Holy Spirit.
Pray for us that we may more completely understand
     and experience
what it means to believe in the Holy Spirit
and to adore him together with the Father and the Son.
     Amen.

XXXI

THE HUMBLE AND GLORIOUS WOMAN

'A great sign appeared in heaven, a woman robed with the sun, with the moon beneath her feet, and at her head a crown of twelve stars. She was pregnant, and in the anguish of her labour she cried out to be delivered. Then a second sign appeared in heaven; a great red dragon with seven heads and ten horns; on his heads were seven diadems, and with his tail he swept down a third of the stars in the sky and flung them to the earth. The dragon stood in front of the woman who was about to give birth, so that when the child was born, he might devour it. She gave birth to a male child, who is destined to rule all nations with an iron rod. But her child was snatched up to God and his throne; and the woman herself fled into the desert where she had a place prepared for her by God, there to be sustained for twelve hundred and sixty days.

'Then war broke out in heaven. Michael and his angels waged war upon the dragon. The dragon and his angels fought, but they had not the strength to win, and no foothold was left for them in heaven. So the great dragon was thrown down, that serpent of old that led the whole world astray, who is called Satan, or the devil — thrown down to the earth, and his angels with him.

'Then I heard a voice in heaven proclaiming aloud: "This is the hour of victory for our God, the hour of his sovereignty and power, when his Christ comes to his rightful rule. For the accuser of our brothers is overthrown, who day and night accused them before God. By the sacrifice of the Lamb, they have conquered him, and by the testimony which they uttered; for they did not hold their lives too dear to lay them down. Rejoice then, you heavens and you who dwell in them".

'When the dragon found that he had been thrown down to the earth, he went in pursuit of the woman who had given birth to the male child. But the woman was given two great eagle's wings to fly to the place in the desert where for three years and a half, she was to be sustained, out of reach of the serpent' (Rev 12: 1-14).

This last Biblical text is somehow a synthesis of all that the Bible has said about Mary. She is presented again as the *Woman,* the Mother of the living, the new Eve. She is the queen of the prophets who lives with intensity the joys, the hopes and the anguish of her people. She is a prophetic sign. This whole text refers at the same time to Mary, the Mother of Jesus, and to the Church. We cannot understand the motherhood of the Church without that of Mary.

The prophetic vision of the Old Testament comes to greater sharpness here. 'The kings of the earth set themselves, and the rulers take counsel together, against the Lord and his anointed . . . I will tell of the decree of the Lord: he said to me, "You are my Son; today I have begotten you. Ask of me, and I will make the nations your heritage" ' (Ps 2: 2-8). Most evident is the reference to the great vision of the book of Genesis about the woman associated with the victory over Satan: 'I will put enmity between you and the woman, and between your seed and her seed' (Gen 3: 15). Mary, who so intensely lived these events, is always present to the Church whose whole history is marked by the same suffering, the same battle, the same hope and victory.

The 'anguish of her labour' is not just a matter of the physical pangs of childbirth. It is all the hope-filled suffering of Mary giving birth to Jesus in the extremes of poverty, the flight into Egypt and all the other experiences of the new exodus right up to the birth of the Church

110

when Christ her Son died on the Cross to send us the Spirit. And at the same time, with the seer of Patmos, we have a vision of the Church, the new Sion, the Mother of the living, who constantly gives birth to new sons and daughters, not without participating in the pangs of Mary's childbirth. The Church sees, before her, her children threatened by the inimical powers which try to devour them as soon as they come to spiritual birth.

'The woman herself fled into the desert'. The prophetic vision of the Book of Revelation reminds us of the flight of the Holy Family into Egypt as a real and prophetic symbol of how God deals with his Church. Again and again, he takes her into the desert. She has to become pure; she is to renounce all earthly securities, all direct and indirect power over the temporal sphere. She cannot share in the final victory of Christ without constantly living the exodus which Jesus has lived with Mary.

'Her child was snatched up to God and his throne'. The almighty Father saved Jesus from the hands of Herod and he finally freed him from the power of death in the paschal victory; he is Lord to the glory of the Father. And we see now the humble woman who throughout her life sings the song of the servant, glorified; the daughter of Sion is the Queen of the apostles; the twelve stars indicate the new family of God represented in the twelve apostles. Her assumption into heaven, her being in the glory of her Son, Jesus Christ, is a divine promise to the Church that she will be exalted if she lives fully the existence of a servant with Christ the Servant, following the example of Mary.

The whole vision of John re-echoes the *Magnificat*: 'The arrogant of heart and mind, he has put to rout, he has brought down monarchs from their thrones, but the humble have been lifted high' (Lk 1:51-52). All the members and office holders of the Church should again and again meditate on how Mary experienced with Jesus the tremendous tension and struggle between two totally opposed messianic expectations. Mary is the leader of

111

those who know that the Messiah is the Servant of God, and that only those can share in his final victory who are willing to follow him in humility, in the poverty that is a gift of the Holy Spirit. On the other side is the earthly expectation of a religion that gives power over others. Jesus has come to drive out this devil: 'Begone, Satan'.

John, the beloved disciple to whom Mary is entrusted in a particular way, speaks here to the Church and announces salvation to her wherever she follows Christ the Servant with his Mother. The Church has no reason to fear insecurity, or the pilgrimage through the desert, as long as she puts all her trust in the Lord. The assumption of Mary into the glory of her Son is an encouragement to the Church to live the detachment, the poverty of the Spirit, and the humility of the servant.

It is impossible to overlook the actuality of this great vision. In this historical hour, the Church is again urged by the Lord to live Advent and the hope of exodus. And, she will live it with the prophetic prayer: 'Maranatha; Come, Lord Jesus'.

We thank you, Father, Lord of heaven and earth,
that you have given your Church the wonderful vision
  of John,
the beloved disciple.
Grant that we may ever better know the Church
as she is prefigured in Mary, the humble handmaid,
  the Queen of the apostles.
Send us your Holy Spirit that we may know Christ,
and in him know you and your design for the Church
  and the world,
and thus share in your life with your Son in the
  Holy Spirit.

O Mary, Queen of the prophets, new Eve,
  Mother of the living,
protect the Church of your Son, Jesus Christ,
  with your prayer and blessing.

Pray for us that we may put all our trust in Jesus Christ, who is your Son and whom you adore as the Son of God, our Lord, our Saviour and our hope. Amen.